T0222760

Frameworkless Front-End Development

Do You Control Your Dependencies or are They Controlling You?

Second Edition

Francesco Strazzullo

Apress®

Frameworkless Front-End Development: Do You Control Your Dependencies or are They Controlling You?

Francesco Strazzullo
TREVISO, Treviso, Italy

ISBN-13 (pbk): 978-1-4842-9350-8   ISBN-13 (electronic): 978-1-4842-9351-5
https://doi.org/10.1007/978-1-4842-9351-5

Managing Director, Apress Media LLC: Welmoed Spahr
Acquisitions Editor: James Robinson-Prior
Development Editor: James Markham
Coordinating Editor: Gryffin Winkler
Copy Editor: Kezia Endsley

Cover image designed by wirestock on Freepik (www.freepik.com)

Distributed to the book trade worldwide by Springer Science+Business Media New York, 233 Spring Street, 6th Floor, New York, NY 10013. Phone 1-800-SPRINGER, fax (201) 348-4505, e-mail orders-ny@springer-sbm.com, or visit www.springeronline.com. Apress Media, LLC is a California LLC and the sole member (owner) is Springer Science + Business Media Finance Inc (SSBM Finance Inc). SSBM Finance Inc is a **Delaware** corporation.

For information on translations, please e-mail booktranslations@springernature.com; for reprint, paperback, or audio rights, please e-mail bookpermissions@springernature.com.

Apress titles may be purchased in bulk for academic, corporate, or promotional use. eBook versions and licenses are also available for most titles. For more information, reference our Print and eBook Bulk Sales web page at http://www.apress.com/bulk-sales.

Any source code or other supplementary material referenced by the author in this book is available to readers on GitHub (https://github.com/Apress). For more detailed information, please visit https://www.apress.com/gp/services/source-code.

Paper in this product is recyclable

To Alessandro, my son.

Table of Contents

About the Author

Francesco Strazzullo is an experienced front-end engineer, JavaScript trainer, developer, and chief operating officer at Claranet Italy. He has presented at tech conferences and meet-ups around Europe. Francesco is a technical reviewer for multiple tech publishers and writes technical articles on his blog. He is always enthusiastic about trying out new APIs, and he firmly believes that the best way to learn something new is to explain and teach it to somebody else. With friends and fellow developers, he founded the Frameworkless Movement, a group interested in developing software without using frameworks and spreading knowledge about making informed decisions about the choice and use of frameworks in front-end software development.

About the Technical Reviewers

Giorgio Boa is a full stack developer; the front-end ecosystem is his passion. He started developing applications in 2006, and in 2012 he fell in love with JavaScript. He is also active in the open-source ecosystem; he loves to learn and study new things. He is very ambitious and tries to improve himself every day.

Luca Del Puppo is a senior software engineer who loves JavaScript and TypeScript. In his free time, he enjoys studying new technologies, improving himself, creating YouTube content, and writing technical articles. He can't live without trail running and loves doing it in his beloved Dolomites.

Acknowledgments

This book was born drinking coffee with my dear friend Lorenzo Massacci. During a coffee break in the office, he asked, "What does it take to make an application last forever?" We never answered that question, but we started thinking about the lifespan of applications and their relationship with frameworks, and we started talking about the frameworkless approach.

I also need to thank Avanscoperta,[1] who helped me prepare my "Frameworkless Front-end Development" workshop and gave me feedback about the frameworkless approach from the attendees, giving me the courage to write down my thoughts.

The last "thank you" goes to my wife Lucia. She does not know anything about JavaScript or frameworks, so she couldn't actually help me write this book. But she does a more important thing. She makes me happy.

---

[1] www.avanscoperta.it/en/training/

The Frameworkless Movement

This book is about two main topics. The first is about working without frameworks effectively; the second is about choosing the right framework for the right project. My friends Antonio Dell'Ava, Lorenzo Massacci, Alessandro Violini and I created the Frameworkless Movement[1] to explore these topics better.

This movement aims to create awareness around these topics, gathering people together in a community. Our main concern is to help people understand that working without a framework is a real possibility nowadays. This book is part of our group's activities to help people understand the importance of technical decision-making. If you're interested and want to be involved, contact us on GitHub.[2]

---

[1] http://frameworklessmovement.org

[2] https://github.com/frameworkless-movement/manifesto

CHAPTER 1

The Definition of Framework

You don't need a framework. You need a painting, not a frame.

—Klaus Kinski

If you are reading this book, you are probably interested in learning how to develop complex applications without relying on—or without relying too *much* on—front-end frameworks.

It would not be smart to start exploring frameworkless solutions without first exploring the meaning of "framework." Consider the first definition of framework by the Cambridge Dictionary:[1]

A supporting structure around which something can be built.

This first and simple definition is consistent with the general idea of a software framework. Think about Angular:[2] it gives you, out-of-the-box, a structure that "supports" your application and a series of elements,

---

[1] https://dictionary.cambridge.org/dictionary/english/framework
[2] https://angular.io/

© Francesco Strazzullo 2023
F. Strazzullo, *Frameworkless Front-End Development*,
https://doi.org/10.1007/978-1-4842-9351-5_1

like `Services`, `Components` and `Pipe`, that can be used to build your applications. However, this simplistic definition is not the only possibility. Let's analyze the definition of framework from other points of view.

Frameworks vs Libraries

It may seem counterintuitive, but a way to easily define frameworks is to highlight their differences from another important part of every codebase: libraries. Without overthinking it, it is safe to say that Angular is a Framework while `lodash` is a library. You can instantly tell the difference between the two tools because of this other definition[3] of framework:

A framework calls your code, your code calls a library.

A framework could internally use one or more libraries, but that fact is usually hidden from the developer, who sees the framework as a single unit, or a bunch of modules if you choose a modular framework. The relationship among application code, frameworks, and libraries can be condensed, as shown in Figure 1-1.

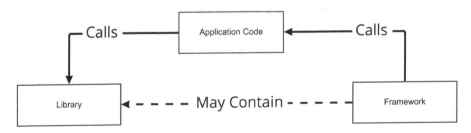

Figure 1-1. *Relationship among frameworks, libraries, and application code*

---

[3] I read this definition often in books or online, but I cannot pinpoint the original source, if there is one.

Comparing Frameworks to Libraries

This section provides several code snippets that illustrate the difference between frameworks and libraries. This comparison uses Angular and date-fns.[4]

Listings 1-1 and 1-2 are basic examples of Component and Service in Angular.

Listing 1-1. Angular Service Example

```
import { Injectable } from '@angular/core'
import { HttpClient } from '@angular/common/http'
import { Observable } from 'rxjs'
import { Order } from './model/order'

const URL = 'http://example.api.com/'

@Injectable({
    providedIn: 'root'
})
export class Orders {
    constructor(private http: HttpClient) {}

    list(): Observable<Order[]> {
        return this.http.get<Order[]>(URL)
    }
}
```

Listing 1-2. Angular Component Example

```
import { Component, OnInit } from '@angular/core'
import { Orders } from '../orders'
import { Order } from '../model/order'
```

---

[4]https://date-fns.org/

3

```
@Component({
  selector: 'app-order-list',
  templateUrl: './order-list.component.html',
  styleUrls: ['./order-list.component.css']
})
export class OrderListComponent implements OnInit {
  list: Order[] = []

  constructor(private orders: Orders) { }

  ngOnInit(): void {
    this.orders.list()
      .subscribe(_orders => this.list = _orders)
  }
}
```

Listing 1-3 is an example of using date-fns to format a date.

Listing 1-3. date-fns Example

```
import { format } from 'date-fns'

const DATE_FORMAT = 'DD/MM/YYYY'

export const formatDate = date => {
    return format(date, DATE_FORMAT)
}
```

The previous definition of the difference between a framework and a library is quite striking when you analyze Listings 1-1 to 1-3. Angular is a framework, and Orders and OrderListComponent will stop working in a codebase without Angular. Angular is calling the application code. If you remove the @Injectable annotation, the service becomes invisible to the Angular code, and the Orders class relies on the HttpClient utility to fulfil its task.

On the other hand, date-fns is not opinionated on how to structure the application's code; you can just import it, and if you respect the public API, you're good to go. Table 1-1 shows a list of libraries grouped by their purpose.

Table 1-1. *Some JavaScript Libraries*

Purpose	Libraries
Utilities	lodash, Ramda
Date manipulation	date-fns, Day.js
Data visualization	D3.js, highcharts, chart.js
Animation	tween.js, anime.js

Frameworks and Decisions

The Cambridge Dictionary provides another definition of framework that is interesting to analyze:

> *A system of rules, ideas, or beliefs that is used to plan or decide something.*

While a "system of rules" is easy to apply to a software framework—every API is a system of rules—the interesting part of this definition is that a system of rules (aka a framework) could be used to decide something. Can software frameworks be used to decide something? The short answer is yes, but let me elaborate on a longer answer. When teams choose to work with a framework, they are deliberately "deciding not to decide" or, to put it in other terms, to let the framework make some decisions for them. Delegating some decisions to another team is not a problem per se, but it may become a problem because these decisions are hidden in plain sight. Mindful teams should analyze these hidden decisions they are delegating and deeply understand their consequences.

Angular's Decisions

To better explain how a framework can make decisions in place of a development team, this section explains the decisions that a team using Angular delegates to the framework.

Language

Using Angular means, first of all, using TypeScript. In the past, you could work with plain JavaScript[5] in an Angular application, but that feature has been removed. TypeScript is a typed superset of JavaScript that compiles to plain JavaScript. Apart from type checking, it also lets you use some features that are not present in the original language, like annotations.

TypeScript can be useful if you and your team are used to working with strongly typed languages. But this also means that if you use Angular, all of your code is written in a language that requires a transpiler.

Observables

Angular is heavily designed around RxJS, a library for reactive programming using observables; in fact, in the previous example, to get the data from `PeopleListService`, you would have to use the `subscribe` method of the `Observable` object. This is a very different approach from the rest of the front-end frameworks, where HTTP requests are designed like promises. Promises provide a standard way to represent the eventual completion (or failure) of an asynchronous operation. RxJS lets you easily transform an `Observable` into a promise[6] and vice versa. But if you need to integrate some promise-based library into your Angular project, you will

---

[5] You can see the breaking change in this commit `https://github.com/angular/angular/commit/cac130eff9b9cb608f2308ae40c42c9cd1850c4d`

[6] "toPromise" is deprecated in favor of "lastValueFrom" `https://indepth.dev/posts/1287/rxjs-heads-up-topromise-is-being-deprecated`

need to do some extra work. For the sake of completeness, this is a similar example using *fetch*,[7] a platform API used to make HTTP requests based on promises. See Listings 1-4 and 1-5.

Listing 1-4. Angular Service without Observables[8]

```
const URL = 'http://example.api.com/'
export class Orders {
    async list(): Promise<Order[]> {
        const response = await fetch(URL)
        const data = await response.json();
        return data;
    }
}
```

Listing 1-5. Angular Component without Observables

```
export class OrderListComponent implements OnInit {
  list: Order[] = []

  constructor(private orders: Orders) { }

  ngOnInit(): void {
    this.orders.list()
      .then(_orders => this.list = _orders)
  }
}
```

Notice that both of these constraints are not bad by themselves; TypeScript and RxJs are both fantastic tools. But the consequences of using these tools (forced by Angular) should be clear to the whole team.

---

[7] https://developer.mozilla.org/en-US/docs/Web/API/fetch
[8] In Listings 1-4 and 1-5, I removed Angular's decorators for the sake of brevity.

The Framework's Way

In these few pages, I have not mentioned the elephant in the room, the most famous tool in the front-end ecosystem: React. This section aims to explain whether React is a framework or a library. The definition of React from the official website[9] is as follows:

A JavaScript library for building user interfaces

It seems easy enough then—React is a library. But the reality is much more complex than that. The main constraint of React is the use of the declarative paradigm. You don't manipulate the DOM, but you modify the state of a component, and then React modifies the DOM for you. This way of programming is also present in most of the libraries of the React ecosystem. The purpose of the snippet in Listing 1-6 is to hide/show a square with an animation. Every time the user presses the Toggle button, using `framer-motion`,[10] it activates an animation library for React. The result is visible in Figure 1-2.

Listing 1-6. framer-motion Animation Example

```
import { useCallback, useState } from 'react';
import { motion } from "framer-motion"

const MotionExample = () => {
    const [isVisible, setIsVisible] = useState(false);
    const toggle = useCallback(() => setIsVisible(!isVisible),
    [isVisible]);

    const opacity = isVisible ? 1 : 0;
```

---

[9] https://reactjs.org/

[10] www.framer.com/docs/introduction/

8

```
    return (
        <div>
            <motion.div
                className='box'
                animate={{ opacity }}
                transition={{
                    ease: 'linear',
                    duration: 0.5
                }}
            />
            <button onClick={toggle}>Toggle</button>
        </div>
    )
}

export default MotionExample
```

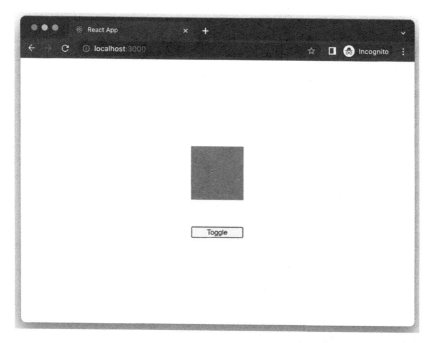

Figure 1-2. *Example of React animation with framed-motion*

As you can see, you don't directly animate the square. You just declare how to map the state with the animation (changing the opacity), and then you change the state. This is the core of the *declarative pattern* used in React. Let's analyze a different approach using a Web Animations API,[11] a standard library used to programmatically create CSS animations. The code shown in Listing 1-7 has the same output as the previous one.

Listing 1-7. Web Animations API Example

```
import { useCallback, useState, useEffect, useRef } from 'react'

const animationTiming = {
    duration: 500,
    ease: 'linear',
    fill: 'forwards'
}

const showKeyframes = [
    { opacity: 0 },
    { opacity: 1 }
]

const hideKeyframes = [
    ...showKeyframes
].reverse()

const show = (element) => {
    element.animate(showKeyframes, animationTiming)
}

const hide = (element) => {
    element.animate(hideKeyframes, animationTiming)
}
```

---

[11] https://developer.mozilla.org/en-US/docs/Web/API/Web_Animations_API

```
const WAExample = () => {
    //using ref to skip a re-render
    const didMountRef = useRef(false);
    const box = useRef(null)
    const [isVisible, setIsVisible] = useState(false)

    const toggle = useCallback(() => {
        setIsVisible(!isVisible)
    }, [isVisible])

    useEffect(() => {
        if(!didMountRef.current) {
            didMountRef.current = true;
            return
        }

        const {
            current
        } = box

        if(isVisible){
            show(current)
        } else{
            hide(current)
        }

    }, [box, isVisible])

    return (
        <div>
            <div
                ref={box}
                className='box'
            />
```

```
        <button onClick={toggle}>Toggle</button>
      </div>
    )
  }
}

export default WAExample
```

The example in Listing 1-6 may seem out of place for a React developer. This is because you're moving the square with an imperative pattern using the animate[12] method of the DOM element. The second example is less "Reacty" than the first one. In other words, when working with React, developers need to consider also a set of unspoken rules imposed not by the API itself but by how the community is using that API. React community-created libraries and tools transform operations that could be imperative in declarative components. In addition to the animation example in Listing 1-6, there are other examples, such as React Router[13] and Apollo Client.[14]

These libraries contributed to creating React's way of writing applications. Every mainstream framework tends to create its framework's way. This aspect leads to the third definition of framework:

If there is a framework's way, there is a framework.

So, following this definition, it becomes crystal clear that React is a framework and not a library. You could use it as a library, but most of the projects will embrace its unspoken rules, making it a framework *de facto*.

As for the Angular rules from the previous paragraph, React's way is not a bad thing per se. But when embracing its declarative way of programming, a team needs to understand what they are gaining and

---

[12] https://developer.mozilla.org/en-US/docs/Web/API/Element/animate
[13] https://reactrouter.com/
[14] www.apollographql.com/docs/react/get-started/

what they are losing. Let's try to do that in Listings 1-6 and 1-7. Both snippets have a similar complexity, but Listing 1-6 is more readable for a React developer because `react-motion` is React-compatible. So, a team that decides to work like in Listing 1-7 is losing readability. But what are they gaining? To answer this question, analyze Listings 1-8 and 1-9; they are slightly different versions of the Web Animations API example from Listing 1-7.

Listing 1-8. Frameworkless Animation Library

```
const animationTiming = {
    duration: 500,
    ease: 'linear',
    fill: 'forwards'
}

const showKeyframes = [
    { opacity: 0 },
    { opacity: 1 }
]

const hideKeyframes = [
    ...showKeyframes
].reverse()

export const show = (element) => {
    element.animate(showKeyframes, animationTiming)
}

export const hide = (element) => {
    element.animate(hideKeyframes, animationTiming)
}
```

Listing 1-9. Web Animations API Example (Revised)

```
import { useCallback, useState, useEffect, useRef } from 'react'
import { show, hide } from './animations'

const WAExample = () => {
    //using ref to skip a re-render
    const didMountRef = useRef(false);
    const box = useRef(null)
    const [isVisible, setIsVisible] = useState(false)

    const toggle = useCallback(() => {
        setIsVisible(!isVisible)
    }, [isVisible])

    useEffect(() => {
        if(!didMountRef.current) {
            didMountRef.current = true;
            return
        }

        const {
            current
        } = box

        if(isVisible){
            show(current)
        } else{
            hide(current)
        }
    }, [box, isVisible])

    return (
        <div>
            <div
```

```
            ref={box}
            className='box'
        />
        <button onClick={toggle}>Toggle</button>
    </div>
    )
}
```

```
export default WAExample
```

It is easy to notice that the only difference with the previous Web Animations API example is that I moved all the animation-related code to a different file. But the code in Listing 1-8 now has an important characteristic: It is completely unrelated to React. It is a simple library without dependencies. This means that it can be used in any kind of JavaScript project without a problem. In this scenario, the team is losing readability but gaining portability.

Tip   When ditching the framework's way, be sure to know *why* you are doing it. The loss of readability, in the long run, could be problematic, so be sure that it is worth it.

Frameworks as Technical Debt

The last definition of framework that I want to share with you is surely bold, even provocative:

Frameworks are technical debt.

Let me elaborate a bit on why I think that every framework is technical debt. When you need to add a feature to a project, you always have options. Some are quick and messy, while others are well-designed but slower to put into production. To better understand the impact of this kind of decision, Ward Cunningham[15] created the metaphor of technical debt. The metaphor itself is quite simple: Every time you choose a quick solution, you incur a debt. A simple diagram of technical debt is shown in Figure 1-3.

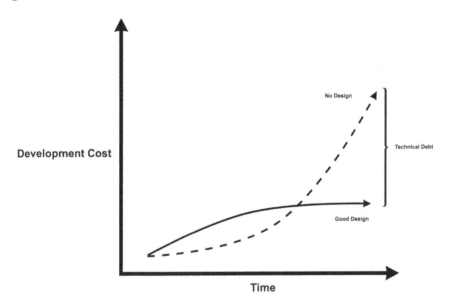

Figure 1-3. *Technical debt*

In the medium term, using a no-design approach will lead to an increase in the cost to add a feature or to change an existing one. This "slowness" is the unpaid debt that a team accumulates over time. When using frameworks, a team starts accumulating the same kind of debt but usually, the slowness comes only in the long term, after some years of active development. In my experience, when an application is

[15] https://youtu.be/pqeJFYwnkjE

commercially successful, its lifespan exceeds the lifespan of frameworks used to build that application. When this happens, the framework is treated like "legacy code," and developers start to struggle and start to slow down development. Just like technical debt.

Technical Investment

Usually, when I tell developers that one of the definitions of framework is technical debt, they think I am an extremist. But I have nothing against frameworks, and—even though I wrote this book—I use frameworks for a large part of my job. My point is that technical debt is not always a bad thing. In the financial world, debt is not automatically a bad thing. For example, to buy a house, you usually get a loan, which is debt. But people tend to not consider the loan a bad thing, but an investment. On the other hand, if a friend of yours without a stable job goes to the bank to get a loan to buy a Ferrari, you might try to stop them.

The difference is not in the debt itself but in the reason behind that debt. Software development has the same kind of mechanism; if you use the no-design solution for a good reason, it is not technical debt, but a *technical investment*. It's always a kind of debt, but it is not reckless. By the same token, frameworks, when chosen for a good reason, are not *costs* but *assets*. *If* you use a framework as an investment, the cost should be eventually paid.

Summary

In this first, introductory, chapter I analyzed four different definitions of framework, and for each one, I tried to highlight what consequences they bring to a developer's daily life.

The next chapter covers a brief history of JavaScript front-end frameworks.

CHAPTER 2

Brief History of Front-end Frameworks

Misunderstanding of the present is the inevitable consequence of ignorance of the past.

—Marc Bloch

This chapter is a very brief history of front-end frameworks. It's not meant to be comprehensive, but it's an opinionated view of the most important milestones in the front-end ecosystem. I divided this chapter into "ages" that contain one or more frameworks. For each age, I explain the ideas that the frameworks of that age introduced to the front-end ecosystem and which ideas are still valid today. Figure 2-1 shows the timeline of the most important frameworks in front-end history.

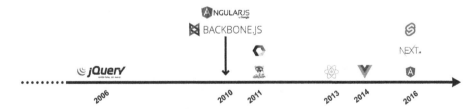

Figure 2-1. *Timeline of front-end frameworks*

The First Age: jQuery

Created by John Resig in 2006, jQuery (see Figure 2-2) the mother of all JavaScript frameworks. It's by far most commonly used[1] in production, with an outstanding 77 percent of the ten million most popular websites.

Figure 2-2. *The jQuery logo*

The most seminal feature of jQuery[2] is the selector syntax, which lets developers select dom nodes with a CSS selector (`var element = $('.my-class')`). The same selector syntax became part of the browsers' platform[3] in 2013.

It may seem strange that this feature became so groundbreaking back then, but you have to consider that at that time, browsers were not aligned as they are today. This is the real value that jQuery brought to the front-end world. jQuery created a *lingua franca* between the browsers. It helped the community grow around common ground. Apart from the selector syntax, during that time a lot of features had been added to the core project, like AJAX requests, animations, and other utilities. It rapidly became the Swiss Army knife of front-end development. Today, developers tend to joke about jQuery and its "ugliness," but it is the cornerstone of modern web development.

---

[1] https://w3techs.com/technologies/overview/javascript_library

[2] https://jquery.com/

[3] https://developer.mozilla.org/en-US/docs/Web/API/Document/querySelector

The jQuery's Way

In the previous chapter, I described the idea of the framework's way. I covered how React is more similar to a framework than a library. From this point of view, jQuery is very similar to React: A library so opinionated and used to become a framework. JQuery's way became evident in 2007 with the advent of jQueryUI,[4] an official UIKit for jQuery applications. This toolkit was easily pluggable, giving developers ready-to-use components for every need. Thanks to the addition of the UI part, jQuery transformed from a utility library to a full-fledged framework. This resonated to other frameworks like AngularJS based on jqlite.

The Second Age: AngularJS, Backbone, and Ember

jQuery gave developers a lot of freedom. Remember that—even if it has its "framework's way"—jQuery is a library that manipulates DOM elements. In the late 2000s, web development frameworks emerged with the Single Page Applications (SPAs) concept. The prominent examples of this era of JavaScript development are AngularJS, Backcone.js, and Ember. All these frameworks implemented the Model View Controller (MVC) pattern or one of its variations. For the sake of brevity, I cover only AngularJS because—in my opinion—it is the one that most influenced the front-end community (see Figure 2-3).

---

[4] https://jqueryui.com/

Figure 2-3. *The AngularJS logo*

AngularJS

If jQuery can be seen as the invention of writing, AngularJS[5] is probably the equivalent of Gutenberg's printing press. AngularJS was developed in 2009 by Miško Hevery[6] as a side project; later, he became a Google employee. Version 1.0 went live on October 20, 2010. It reached its end-of-life[7] on December 31, 2021. AngularJS had huge success and helped make SPAs a mainstream pattern. The main—and most infamous—characteristic of AngularJS is its two-way data binding. Every update in the model updates the view, and every update in the view updates the model. A simple schema of two-way data binding is shown in Figure 2-4.

---

[5] https://angularjs.org/

[6] https://en.wikipedia.org/wiki/AngularJS#Development_history

[7] https://blog.angular.io/discontinued-long-term-support-for-angularjs-cc066b82e65a

Change in Model updates the View

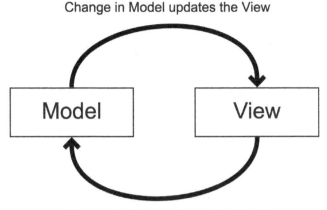

Change in View updates the Model

Figure 2-4. *Two-way data binding*

To better understand how this mechanism works, Listing 2-1 shows an example of ngModel, the most commonly used AngularJS construct. The example is adapted from the official AngularJS documentation.[8]

Listing 2-1. AngularJS Two-Way Data Binding Example

```
<script>
 angular.module('inputExample', [])
.controller('ExampleController', ['$scope', function($scope) {
    $scope.val = '1';
}]);
</script>
<form ng-controller="ExampleController">
  <input ng-model="val" />
</form>
```

---

[8] https://docs.angularjs.org/api/ng/directive/ngModel

The value in the `input` element is bound to the value in `$scope.val`, so the initial value is '1.' When the user changes the value in the `input`, the value of `$scope.val` changes accordingly. When this approach was presented, it generated quite a "wow effect" and quickly became the reason that people chose to work with AngularJS. Nevertheless, this approach started to feel "stale" after some time. Binding the model and the view in this way is not a good option for large codebases, where complex data transformation is needed because overusing this technique slows down the application. AngularJS introduced components and one-way data bindings in later releases, but its popularity decreased, and it has been replaced by modern frameworks.

The Third Age: React, Angular, and Vue

Enter the modern age of front-end development. While I'm writing this chapter—in 2023—the front-end ecosystem is dominated by three players: Angular, React, and Vue. In this case, I do not discuss the consequences because these frameworks are still widely used today. In this section, I analyze just the first two because I think that they represent two different ways of thinking—in fact they are poles apart—about front-end development.

Angular

Angular[9] was previously known as Angular2 because the project was intended to be the new version of AngularJS. The team behind the project took semantic versioning very seriously, thus Angular2 was a completely different framework, as you saw in the previous pages. Such a different approach between the two versions caused a wave of panic around the project. After the first release of Angular2 in September 2016, the team decided to rename the project Angular (see Figure 2-5).

---

[9] https://angular.io/

Figure 2-5. *The Angular logo*

Thanks to a collaboration between Google and Microsoft, its development seemed quite troubled initially. At first, Angular's team announced that the framework used AtScript,[10] a dedicated language created specifically for Angular. Later, the team switched to TypeScript, a new language developed by Microsoft. Angular was built with corporate companies in mind. With the advent of AngularJS, many companies created SPAs thanks to the framework. But AngularJS was not ready for huge codebases. The use of TypeScript, ideas borrowed from other ecosystems—such as annotations for dependency injection—and stable release planning are probably the main reasons behind the success of Angular.

---

[10] The name "AtScript" comes from the @ ("at") symbol used for annotations in many languages and frameworks, like Java Spring.

React

React[11] (see Figure 2-6) was created internally at Facebook in 2011 and released publicly in 2013. React made the concept of the "component" mainstream in the front-end ecosystem, probably thanks to the adoption of JSX, which lets developers use HTML tags in JavaScript files.

Figure 2-6. *The React logo*

Another React characteristic that changed the way people work with data in front-end applications was one-way data binding, also thanks to external libraries like Redux. This approach was revolutionary at the time compared to AngularJS' standard two-way data binding. Thanks to React and its community concept, data immutability became widely used in the front-end ecosystem.

---

[11] https://reactjs.org/

Comparing Angular and React

At the beginning of this section, I said that Angular and React are poles apart. Nevertheless, they are constantly compared in talks, blog posts, and so on. I usually find these comparisons quite unuseful because they don't give readers a complete picture. I do not compare them in this paragraph, but I do highlight the most important difference between the two frameworks. Angular is built "in a laboratory" with the purpose of becoming a popular framework, while React is created and maintained mostly by Facebook to solve its problems. This "political" aspect is reflected in the structure of the two frameworks. On one hand, Angular may feel "too big" and almost bloated for some scenarios, but it has a stable API and a defined roadmap.

On the other hand, React is smaller and leaner and thus easier to integrate with custom or existent code. But React's API is less stable between versions compared to Angular. The advent of *hooks*[12] completely changed the way React applications are built; this aspect instills fear in some companies that require stability in the tools that they use.

Bonus Tracks

In this last section of this chapter, I briefly cover some other technologies that did not (yet) have the same impact on the front-end ecosystem, but that I find interesting, nevertheless.

Web Components

Not a framework, but a significant step in front-end history, web components are a set of native APIs that let developers build custom HTML components without any dependencies. They were introduced

---

[12] https://reactjs.org/docs/hooks-intro.html

to the public by Alex Russell at the Frontiers Conference in 2011.[13] In the last period, libraries like `Lit` or `Stencil` are becoming more common in front-end ecosystems because they improve and make it easier to build `WebComponent`. Chapter 4 covers them deeply, explaining how to leverage them to create UI components.

Svelte

The "disappearing frameworks" way has become a recent phenomenon in the front-end ecosystem. In this category, frameworks are reactive by design. During the compilation process, the framework translates syntax in vanilla JavaScript to be lightweight and fully reactive at runtime, so the library payload effectively "disappears" apart from some core functions. The most famous framework in this category is Svelte (see Figure 2-7).[14]

---

[13] https://fronteers.nl/congres/2011/sessions/web-components-and-model-driven-views-alex-russell

[14] https://svelte.dev/

Figure 2-7. *The Svelte logo*

Apart from the fact that you don't serve the whole library payload, a vanilla JavaScript approach is a great way to inject Svelte into existing applications. As you will see in Chapter 4, the main advantage of web components is that they act exactly as standard HTML elements, making this kind of integration frictionless.

Next.JS

From a high-level point of view, single page applications (SPAs) are just empty pages until the JS Framework kicks in and starts rendering content. This approach is unsuitable for SEO because spiders can't grasp the content of JS-generated elements. React enabled server-side rendering (SSR), but doing SSR with pure React on a node server is quite cumbersome. Next.JS[15] solves this problem with an all-in-one solution that builds an SSR-ready application and the possibility to build a set of REST APIs within the same project of the React application. Thanks to the acquisition by Vercel,[16] it is possible to deploy a working React application (with SSR) in minutes. See Figure 2-8.

Another important concept built in to Next.JS is ISR[17] (incremental static render). This approach allows building and keeping one or more pages in the cache for a specific time. The system rebuilds the page with the new data at expiration, and the cycle continues until the server runs. This approach permits you to reduce the cost of the page's creation and the cost of the computation on the server. It's also possible to re-create pages on demand if you need them before the cache expires.

Figure 2-8. *Next.JS logo*

---

[15] https://nextjs.org/

[16] https://vercel.com/

[17] https://nextjs.org/docs/pages/building-your-application/data-fetching/incremental-static-regeneration

Summary

This chapter summarized a very brief history of front-end development, highlighting the tools that I find are the most important and "seminal" in the recent past. I also pointed out some frameworks that I think are worth watching and analyzing for their growth.

The next chapter covers the frameworkless way to build a rendering engine.

CHAPTER 3

Rendering

One of the most important features of any web application is the ability to display data. On a more "close to the metal" level, displaying data means *rendering elements to the screen* or another output device. The World Wide Web Consortium defines rendering elements programmatically with the *Document Object Model*, also known as the DOM. This chapter aims to teach you how to effectively manipulate DOM without frameworks.

The Document Object Model

The Document Object Model (DOM) is how the World Wide Web Consortium (W3C) defines how to interact with HTML documents. Basically, the DOM is an API that lets you manipulate the elements that compose a web application.[1]

To understand the DOM, return to the basics: What is an HTML page? From a technical standpoint, every HTML page (or fragment of one) is a tree. If you have an HTML table like the one in Listing 3-1, its DOM representation will be the one shown in Figure 3-1.

---

[1] You can read more about it on the official W3C specification page at `www.w3.org/ TR/1998/WD-DOM-19980720/introduction.html`.

© Francesco Strazzullo 2023
F. Strazzullo, *Frameworkless Front-End Development*,
https://doi.org/10.1007/978-1-4842-9351-5_3

Listing 3-1. Simple HTML Table

```
<html>
<body>
  <table>
    <tr>
      <th>Framework</th>
      <th>GitHub Stars</th>
    </tr>
    <tr>
      <td>Vue</td>
      <td>118917</td>
    </tr>
    <tr>
      <td>React</td>
      <td>115392</td>
    </tr>
  </table>
</body>
</html>
```

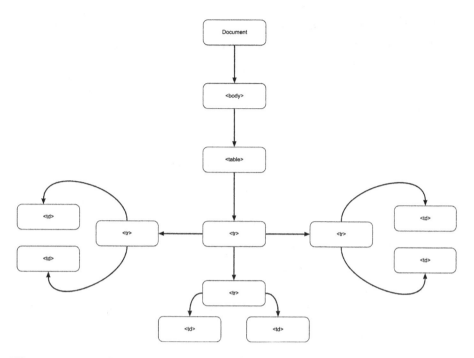

Figure 3-1. *DOM representation of a table*

With this example, it becomes clear that the DOM is a way to manage the tree defined by your HTML elements. So if you want to change the background color of a React cell, you can write something like Listing 3-2.

Listing 3-2. Changing the Color of a React cell

```
const SELECTOR = 'tr:nth-child(3) > td'
const cell =  document.querySelector(SELECTOR)
cell.style.backgroundColor = 'red'
```

The code is quite straightforward. You select the right cell with the `querySelector` method using a standard CSS selector, and change the `style` property of the cell node. The `querySelector` method is just one of the methods of `Node`, the basic interface that represents a node in your HTML tree.[2]

Monitoring Rendering Performance

When designing a rendering engine for the web, you should keep in mind *readability* and *maintainability*. Rendering is such an important task of any web application that, if you decide to write it from scratch, it should be very easy to understand and change.

Another important factor for a rendering engine is performance. This section explains tools you can use to monitor the performance of your rendering engine.

Chrome Developer Tools

The first tool that you are going to use is the browser, more specifically Chrome and its well-known developer tools. One of the features that you can use to monitor rendering performances is a handy frame per second (FPS) meter. To make it appear, press Cmd/Ctrl+Shift+P while the Developer tools are open to show the Command menu, as shown in Figure 3-2. There, choose the Show Frame Per Seconds (FPS) Meter option.

---

[2] You can read all its methods and properties on the Mozilla Developer Network page about it at `https://developer.mozilla.org/en-US/docs/Web/API/Node`.

Figure 3-2. *The Chrome Command menu*

The FPS meter will appear in the upper-right corner of the screen. It will also display the amount of memory used by the GPU, as you can see in Figure 3-3.

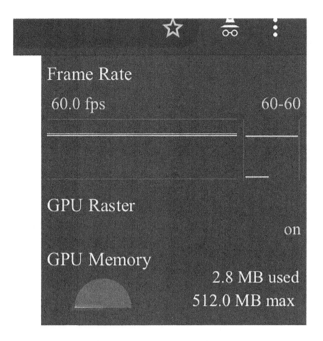

Figure 3-3. *Chrome FPS meter*

The stats.js Widget

Another way to monitor the FPS of your application is to use stats.js,[3] a library that is easy to embed into any web application. Apart from FPS, this tool can also display the milliseconds needed to render a frame or MBytes of allocated memory. In the Readme file in the GitHub repository, you may also find a simple bookmarklet to attach the widget to *any* website, like the one shown in Figure 3-4.

---

[3] https://github.com/mrdoob/stats.js/

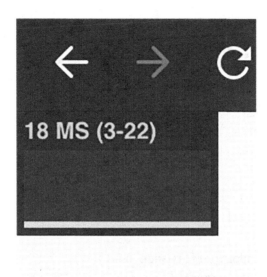

Figure 3-4. *The stats.js widget showing ms needed to render a frame*

Custom Performance Widget

Creating a widget that shows the FPS of your application is quite easy. The main concept is to use the `requestAnimationFrame` callback to track the time between one render cycle and the next one and to keep track of how many times the callback is invoked in a second. You can see an example in Listing 3-3.

Listing 3-3. Custom Performance Monitor Widget

```
let panel
let start
let frames = 0

const create = () => {
  const div = document.createElement('div')

  div.style.position = 'fixed'
```

```
  div.style.left = '0px'
  div.style.top = '0px'
  div.style.width = '50px'
  div.style.height = '50px'
  div.style.backgroundColor = 'black'
  div.style.color = 'white'

  return div
}

const tick = () => {
  frames++
  const now = window.performance.now()
  if (now >= start + 1000) {
    panel.innerText = frames
    frames = 0
    start = now
  }
  window.requestAnimationFrame(tick)
}

const init = (parent = document.body) => {
  panel = create()

  window.requestAnimationFrame(() => {
    start = window.performance.now()
    parent.appendChild(panel)
    tick()
  })
}

export default {
  init
}
```

After calculating the FPS, you can display the number on a widget, as in this case, or use the console to print the data.

Rendering Functions

This section analyzes various ways to render elements to the DOM with pure functions. Rendering elements with pure functions means that the DOM elements depend exclusively on the application's state. To grasp this concept from a formal point of view, consider Figure 3-5.

$$view = f(state)$$

Figure 3-5. *A mathematical representation of pure functions rendering*

You will learn about the "state" of your application and how to manage it in Chapter 8, which covers state management.

There are a lot of advantages to using pure functions, like testability and composability. Still, as you will see later in this chapter, some challenges need to be discussed.

TodoMVC

The example in this chapter uses a TodoMVC template as a base. TodoMVC[4] is a project that collects many implementations of the same to-do list written with different frameworks.[5] Figure 3-6 shows a standard TodoMVC application.

---

[4] http://todomvc.com/

[5] You can see a live demo of a TodoMVC implementation at http://todomvc.com/examples/react/#/.

41

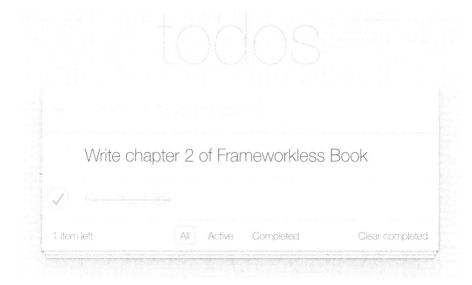

Figure 3-6. *TodoMVC example*

For now, you will concentrate on rendering: You will render the items and the toolbar. In the later chapters, you will add other elements like HTTP requests, event handling, and so on, until you can create a complete application.

Rendering Pure Functions

In this first example, you will use strings to render elements. You can see the skeleton of a TodoMVC application in the next snippet.[6] Listing 3-4 shows the contents of the `index.html` file.

---

[6]You can read the complete code of this example at `https://github.com/Apress/Frameworkless-Front-End-Development-2nd-ed./tree/main/Chapter03/01`.

Listing 3-4. Basic TodoMVC App Structure

```
<body>
  <section class="todoapp">
    <header class="header">
      <h1>todos</h1>
      <input
        class="new-todo"
        placeholder="What needs to be done?">
    </header>
    <section class="main">
      <input
        id="toggle-all"
        class="toggle-all"
        type="checkbox">
      <label for="toggle-all">
        Mark all as complete
      </label>
      <ul class="todo-list"></ul>
    </section>
    <footer class="footer">
      <span class="todo-count"></span>
      <ul class="filters">
        <li>
          <a href="#/">All</a>
        </li>
        <li>
          <a href="#/active">Active</a>
        </li>
```

```
        <li>
          <a href="#/completed">Completed</a>
        </li>
      </ul>
      <button class="clear-completed">
        Clear completed
      </button>
    </footer>
  </section>
  <footer class="info">
    <p>Double-click to edit a todo</p>
  </footer>
</body>
```

To make this application *dynamic*, you need to grab the to-do list data and update it:

- The ul with the list of filtered to-dos

- The span with the number of not completed to-dos

- The links with filter types, adding the selected class to the right one

Listing 3-5 is the first attempt at functional rendering.

Listing 3-5. The First Version of a TodoMVC Rendering Function

```
const getTodoElement = todo => {
  const {
    text,
    completed
  } = todo
```

```
    return `
    <li ${completed ? 'class="completed"' : ''}>
      <div class="view">
        <input
          ${completed ? 'checked' : ''}
          class="toggle"
          type="checkbox">
        <label>${text}</label>
        <button class="destroy"></button>
      </div>
      <input class="edit" value="${text}">
    </li>`
}

const getTodoCount = todos => {
  const notCompleted = todos
    .filter(todo => !todo.completed)

  const { length } = notCompleted
  if (length === 1) {
    return '1 Item left'
  }

  return `${length} Items left`
}

export default (targetElement, state) => {
  const {
    currentFilter,
    todos
  } = state
```

```
const element = targetElement.cloneNode(true)

const list = element.querySelector('.todo-list')
const counter = element.querySelector('.todo-count')
const filters = element.querySelector('.filters')

list.innerHTML = todos.map(getTodoElement).join('')
counter.textContent = getTodoCount(todos)

Array
  .from(filters.querySelectorAll('li a'))
  .forEach(a => {
    if (a.textContent === currentFilter) {
      a.classList.add('selected')
    } else {
      a.classList.remove('selected')
    }
  })
  return element
}
```

This view function takes a target DOM element as a base. It then clones the original node and updates it using the state parameter. It then returns the new node. Notice that these DOM modifications are *virtual*; you are working with a *detached* element. To create a detached element, you clone an existing node with the cloneNode method. This newly created DOM element is an exact clone of a real DOM element but is completely unrelated to the document's body.

So, in Listing 3-5, no real modifications to the DOM are committed. Keep in mind that modifying a detached DOM element is quite performant. To connect this view function to the real DOM, you can use a simple controller like the one in Listing 3-6.

Listing 3-6. Basic Controller

```
import getTodos from './getTodos.js'
import view from './view.js'

const state = {
  todos: getTodos(),
  currentFilter: 'All'
}

const main = document.querySelector('.todoapp')

window.requestAnimationFrame(() => {
  const newMain = view(main, state)
  main.replaceWith(newMain)
})
```

This simple "rendering engine" is based on requestAnimationFrame.[7] Every DOM manipulation or animation should be based on this DOM API. Making DOM operations inside this callback makes everything more efficient; they don't block the main thread and they are executed right before the next repaint is scheduled in the event loop.[8]

This data model is a random array generated with Faker.js,[9] a small library useful for generating random data. In Figure 3-7, you can see the schema of the first rendering example.

---

[7] https://developer.mozilla.org/en-US/docs/Web/API/window/requestAnimationFrame

[8] To better understand how the event loop works, I suggest watching this talk by Jake Archibald (https://vimeo.com/254947206).

[9] https://fakerjs.dev/

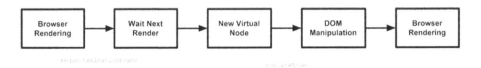

Figure 3-7. Static rendering schema

Reviewing the Code

This rendering approach is performant enough using requestAnimationFrame and virtual node manipulation. But this view function is not very readable. That code[10] has two major problems:

- **It's just a single huge function**: You have a single function to manipulate different DOM elements. The situation can easily become messy.

- **There are different approaches to doing the same thing**: You create list items via strings. You just add the text to an existing element for the todo count element. For the filters, you manage the classList.

In the next example, you see how to divide the view into smaller functions and try to address the consistency problem.

Listing 3-7 shows the refactored version of this application, while Listings 3-8, 3-9, and 3-10 show the new functions for the counter, the filters, and the list, respectively.

---

[10] You can find the complete code of this second version at https://github.com/
Apress/Frameworkless-Front-End-Development-2nd-ed./tree/main/
Chapter03/02.

Listing 3-7. App View Function with Smaller View Functions

```
import todosView from './todos.js'
import counterView from './counter.js'
import filtersView from './filters.js'

export default (targetElement, state) => {
  const element = targetElement.cloneNode(true)

  const list = element
    .querySelector('.todo-list')
  const counter = element
    .querySelector('.todo-count')
  const filters = element
    .querySelector('.filters')

  list.replaceWith(todosView(list, state))
  counter.replaceWith(counterView(counter, state))
  filters.replaceWith(filtersView(filters, state))

  return element
}
```

Listing 3-8. View Function to Show the Count of Todos

```
const getTodoCount = todos => {
  const notCompleted = todos
    .filter(todo => !todo.completed)

  const { length } = notCompleted
  if (length === 1) {
    return '1 Item left'
  }

  return `${length} Items left`
}
```

```
export default (targetElement, { todos }) => {
  const newCounter = targetElement.cloneNode(true)
  newCounter.textContent = getTodoCount(todos)
  return newCounter
}
```

Listing 3-9. The View Function to Render the TodoMVC Filters

```
export default (targetElement, { currentFilter }) => {
  const newCounter = targetElement.cloneNode(true)
  Array
    .from(newCounter.querySelectorAll('li a'))
    .forEach(a => {
      if (a.textContent === currentFilter) {
        a.classList.add('selected')
      } else {
        a.classList.remove('selected')
      }
    })
  return newCounter
}
```

Listing 3-10. The View Function to Render the List

```
const getTodoElement = todo => {
  const {
    text,
    completed
  } = todo

  return `
      <li ${completed ? 'class="completed"' : ''}>
        <div class="view">
          <input
```

```
            ${completed ? 'checked' : ''}
            class="toggle"
            type="checkbox">
         <label>${text}</label>
         <button class="destroy"></button>
       </div>
       <input class="edit" value="${text}">
     </li>`
}

export default (targetElement, { todos }) => {
  const newTodoList = targetElement.cloneNode(true)
  const todosElements = todos
    .map(getTodoElement)
    .join('')
  newTodoList.innerHTML = todosElements
  return newTodoList
}
```

The code is much better now; you have three separate functions with the same signature. These functions are the first draft of a *component library.*

Component Functions

If you check the code of the app view (see Listing 3-7), you need to *manually* invoke the right function. If you want to create a component-based application, you should use a declarative way of interaction between components. The system should automatically wire all the pieces.

The next application[11] is an example of a rendering engine with a component registry. To achieve this goal, the first thing that you should do is define how to declare what component should be used in a particular use case. In this particular scenario, you have three components: *todos*, a *counter,* and *filters*. Listing 3-11 defines which component should be used by using data-attributes.[12]

Listing 3-11. App Using Data Attributes to Determine Component Use

```
<section class="todoapp">
    <header class="header">
        <h1>todos</h1>
        <input
            class="new-todo"
            placeholder="What needs to be done?"
            autofocus>
    </header>
    <section class="main">
        <input
            id="toggle-all"
            class="toggle-all"
            type="checkbox">
        <label for="toggle-all">
            Mark all as complete
        </label>
```

---

[11] https://github.com/Apress/Frameworkless-Front-End-Development-2nd-ed./tree/main/Chapter03/03

[12] https://developer.mozilla.org/en-US/docs/Learn/HTML/Howto/Use_data_attributes

```
    <ul class="todo-list" data-component="todos">
    </ul>
</section>
<footer class="footer">
    <span
        class="todo-count"
        data-component="counter">
            1 Item Left
    </span>
    <ul class="filters" data-component="filters">
        <li>
            <a href="#/">All</a>
        </li>
        <li>
            <a href="#/active">Active</a>
        </li>
        <li>
            <a href="#/completed">Completed</a>
        </li>
    </ul>
    <button class="clear-completed">
        Clear completed
    </button>
</footer>
</section>
```

In the previous snippet, the "name" of the component is in the data-component attribute. This attribute will replace the imperative invocation of view functions. Another prerequisite needed to create a component library is a *registry*: An index of all the components available in the application. The simplest registry that you can implement is a plain JavaScript object like the one shown in Listing 3-12.

Listing 3-12. Simple Component Registry

```
const registry = {
  'todos': todosView,
  'counter': counterView,
  'filters': filtersView
}
```

The keys of this registry tally with the value of the `data-component` attribute. This is the key mechanism of the component-based rendering engine. This mechanism should be applied not only to the root container (the application view function) but also to every component that you will create. In this way, every component can be used inside other components. This kind of reusability is required for every component-based application. In order to accomplish this task, every component should "inherit" from a base component that reads the values of the `data-component` attribute and automatically invoke the right function. Given that these are pure functions, you can't really inherit from a base object. So you need to create a high-order function that wraps these components. You can see an example of this kind of high-order function in Listing 3-13.

Listing 3-13. Rendering a High-Order Function

```
const renderWrapper = component => {
  return (targetElement, state) => {
    const element = component(targetElement, state)

    const childComponents = element
      .querySelectorAll('[data-component]')

    Array
      .from(childComponents)
      .forEach(target => {
        const name = target
```

```
        .dataset
        .component

      const child = registry[name]
      if (!child) {
        return
      }

      target.replaceWith(child(target, state))
    })

    return element
  }
}
```

This wrapper function takes the original component and returns a new component with the same signature. To the system, the two functions are identical. For every DOM element with the data-component attribute, the wrapper looks for it in the registry. If it finds something, it will invoke the child component. But also this child component is wrapped with the same function. In this way, you can easily navigate all the way down to the last component, just like a recursive function does.

So, to add a component to the registry, you need a simple function that wraps a component with the previous function, like the one shown in Listing 3-14.

Listing 3-14. Registry Accessor Method

```
const add = (name, component) => {
  registry[name] = renderWrapper(component)
}
```

You should also provide a method to render the root of the application to start rendering from an initial DOM element. In this application, this method is called renderRoot, and you can see its code in Listing 3-15.

Listing 3-15. Boot Function of a Component-Based Application

```
const renderRoot = (root, state) => {
  const cloneComponent = root => {
    return root.cloneNode(true)
  }

  return renderWrapper(cloneComponent)(root, state)
}
```

The add and renderRoot methods are the public interfaces of the component registry. The last thing to do is mix all the elements in the controller, as shown in Listing 3-16.

Listing 3-16. A Controller That Uses a Component Registry

```
import getTodos from './getTodos.js'
import todosView from './view/todos.js'
import counterView from './view/counter.js'
import filtersView from './view/filters.js'

import registry from './registry.js'

registry.add('todos', todosView)
registry.add('counter', counterView)
registry.add('filters', filtersView)

const state = {
  todos: getTodos(),
  currentFilter: 'All'
}
```

```
window.requestAnimationFrame(() => {
  const main = document.querySelector('.todoapp')
  const newMain = registry.renderRoot(main, state)
  main.replaceWith(newMain)
})
```

That's it! You just created your first frameworkless component-based application. You can consider it a *walking skeleton*[13] of a real component-based application. You can see a basic schema of this application in Figure 3-8.

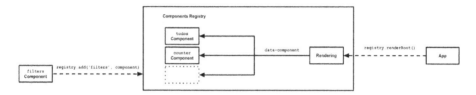

Figure 3-8. *Component registry schema*

Rendering Dynamic Data

In the previous examples, you used static data. But in a real-world application, data will change over time because of an event from the user or the system. You will learn about event listeners in the next chapter, so for now, you can just change the state randomly every five seconds, as you can see in Listing 3-17.

---

[13] https://gojko.net/2014/06/09/forget-the-walking-skeleton-put-it-on-crutches/

Listing 3-17. Rendering Random Data Every Five Seconds

```
const render = () => {
  window.requestAnimationFrame(() => {
    const main = document.querySelector('.todoapp')
    const newMain = registry.renderRoot(main, state)
    main.replaceWith(newMain)
  })
}

window.setInterval(() => {
  state.todos = getTodos()
  render()
}, 5000)

render()
```

Every time you have new data, you just create another virtual root element and then replace the real one with the newly created one. This could be performant enough for a small application like this one, but in a non-trivial project, this approach would be a *performance killer*.

The Virtual DOM

The virtual DOM approach, made famous by React, is a way to make a declarative rendering engine, like the one that you created, performant. The main idea is that the representation of the UI is kept in memory and synced with the "real" DOM doing the minimum number of operations possible. This process is called *reconciliation*. As an example, if your "old" real DOM element is this simple list.

```
<ul>
  <li>First Item</li>
</ul>
```

You want to replace it with a new list with a new element like this one:

```
<ul>
  <li>First Item</li>
  <li>Second Item</li>
</ul>
```

With the previous algorithm, you replace the entire ul. With the virtual DOM method, the system should dynamically understand that the only operation that is needed on the real DOM is the addition of the last li. The core of the virtual DOM is a diff algorithm that easily understands the fastest way to turn the real DOM into an exact copy of the new DOM element that is detached (in other words, virtual) from the document. A visual explanation of this mechanism is shown in Figure 3-9.

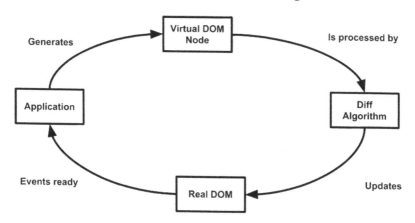

Figure 3-9. *Virtual DOM*

A Simple Virtual DOM Implementation

You can create a very simple diff algorithm to use instead of replaceWith in the main controller, as shown in Listing 3-18.

Listing 3-18. The Main Controller Built with a diff Algorithm

```
const render = () => {
  window.requestAnimationFrame(() => {
    const main = document.querySelector('.todoapp')
    const newMain = registry.renderRoot(main, state)
    applyDiff(document.body, main, newMain)
  })
}
```

The applyDiff function parameters are the parent of the current real DOM node, the real DOM node, and the new virtual DOM node. Let's analyze what this function should do.

You first need to remove the real node if the new node is not defined.

```
if (realNode && !virtualNode) {
  realNode.remove()
}
```

On the other hand, if the real node is not defined but a virtual one exists, you should add it to the parent node.

```
if (!realNode && virtualNode) {
  parentNode.appendChild(virtualNode)
}
```

If both nodes are defined, you need to determine there are differences between them.

```
if (isNodeChanged(virtualNode, realNode)) {
  realNode.replaceWith(virtualNode)
}
```

You are going to analyze the code of the isNodeChanged function in a moment. You first need to apply the same diff algorithm to every child node.

```
const realChildren = Array.from(realNode.children)
const virtualChildren = Array.from(virtualNode.children)

const max = Math.max(
  realChildren.length,
  virtualChildren.length
)
for (let i = 0; i < max; i++) {
  applyDiff(
    realNode,
    realChildren[i],
    virtualChildren[i]
  )
}
```

The complete code of the applyDiff function is shown in Listing 3-19, while Listing 3-20 shows the code of the isNodeChanged function.

Listing 3-19. The applyDiff Function

```
const applyDiff = (
  parentNode,
  realNode,
  virtualNode) => {
  if (realNode && !virtualNode) {
    realNode.remove()
    return
  }
```

```
  if (!realNode && virtualNode) {
    parentNode.appendChild(virtualNode)
    return
  }

  if (isNodeChanged(virtualNode, realNode)) {
    realNode.replaceWith(virtualNode)
    return
  }

  const realChildren = Array.from(realNode.children)
  const virtualChildren = Array.from(virtualNode.children)

  const max = Math.max(
    realChildren.length,
    virtualChildren.length
  )
  for (let i = 0; i < max; i++) {
    applyDiff(
      realNode,
      realChildren[i],
      virtualChildren[i]
    )
  }
}
```

Listing 3-20. The isNodeChanged Function

```
const isNodeChanged = (node1, node2) => {
  const n1Attributes = node1.attributes
  const n2Attributes = node2.attributes
  if (n1Attributes.length !== n2Attributes.length) {
    return true
  }
```

```
const differentAttribute = Array
  .from(n1Attributes)
  .find(attribute => {
    const { name } = attribute
    const attribute1 = node1
      .getAttribute(name)
    const attribute2 = node2
      .getAttribute(name)
    return attribute1 !== attribute2
  })

if (differentAttribute) {
  return true
}

if (node1.children.length === 0 &&
  node2.children.length === 0 &&
  node1.textContent !== node2.textContent) {
  return true
}

return false
}
```

In this implementation of a diff algorithm, you perform these checks to decide if a node has changed compared to another one:

- The number of attributes is different

- There is at least one attribute that has changed

- The nodes have no children and their textContent is different

You can create more refined checks in order to increase performance, but I suggest keeping the rendering engine as simple as possible. Keep an eye on performance using one of the tools at the beginning of the chapter and when a problem arises, try to adapt your algorithm to your use case. Quoting Donald Knuth:[14]

> *Premature optimization is the root of all evil (or at least most of it) in programming.*

Summary

In this chapter, you learned how to create a rendering engine for a frameworkless application. You also explored how to build a simple component registry and how to make your engine perform well by using a virtual DOM algorithm.

In the next chapter, you learn how to manage events from the user and how to integrate these events into the rendering engine.

---

[14] https://en.wikipedia.org/wiki/Donald_Knuth

CHAPTER 4

Managing DOM Events

In the last chapter, you learned about rendering or, more generally, how to *draw* DOM elements that match your data. *But a web application is not a painting; its contents change over time.* The cause of these changes is *events.*

Events, even though they are created by the user or the system, are a crucial aspect of the DOM API. This chapter aims to explain how to manage these events in a frameworkless application.

The first part of the chapter is an introduction to the DOM Events API. You will learn what an event handler is and how to attach it to DOM elements properly. In the second part, you will add interactivity to managing events in your TodoMVC application.

The YAGNI Principle

In this chapter, you will modify the rendering engine from the previous chapter to add the DOM events management. So, why did I show you an incomplete engine, completely ignoring the events? Some of the reasons are readability and simplicity. But I would use the same approach for a real-world project. I would start focusing on the most important feature and then iterate, evolving my architecture around new needs. This is one

© Francesco Strazzullo 2023
F. Strazzullo, *Frameworkless Front-End Development,*
https://doi.org/10.1007/978-1-4842-9351-5_4

of the principles of Extreme Programming (XP) called *YAGNI* (You aren't Gonna Need It). To better explain the *YAGNI* principle, I often use this quote from Ron Jeffries,[1] one of the founders of XP.

> *Always implement things when you actually need them, never when you just foresee that you will need them.*

This principle is good for any use case, but it is crucial for a frameworkless project. When I talk about the frameworkless approach, one of the criticisms that I hear often is, "You will just write another framework that no one will maintain." This is a risk if you overengineer your architecture. When you're creating your own architecture, you should apply *YAGNI* very strictly, solving only the problems that you have at that moment, and not trying to foresee the future.

Look at how I wrote the code in the last chapter as a reference for the *YAGNI* principle. I (tried to) write the best code possible for rendering, and only later I added the events to the mix.

The DOM Events API

Events are actions in a web application that the browser tells you about so that you can *react* to them in some way. There is a wide variety of event types, and you can consult the Mozilla Developer Network for a comprehensive list.[2]

You can react to events triggered by the use, such as mouse events (click, double-click, etc.), keyboard events (keydown, keyup, etc.), view events (resize, scroll, etc.), and so on. Furthermore, the system itself can emit events. For example, it can react to changes in your network status or when the DOM content is loaded, as shown in Figure 4-1.

---

[1]`https://ronjeffries.com/`

[2]`https://developer.mozilla.org/en-US/docs/Web/Events`

Figure 4-1. *Basic click event lifecycle*

To react to an event, you need to attach a special callback, called an *event handler,* to the DOM element that triggered the event.

Tip   For view or system events, attach the event handler to the window object.

Attach Handlers with Properties

A quick and dirty way to attach an event handler to a DOM element is using the on* properties. Every event type has a corresponding property on the DOM elements. A button has the onclick property, but also ondblclick, onmouseover, onblur, onfocus, and so on. It's quite straightforward to attach a handler to a click event using properties, as shown in Listing 4-1. The result of this listing is visible in Figure 4-2.

Listing 4-1.   Click Handler with onclick Property

```
const button = document.querySelector('button')
button.onclick = () => {
  console.log('Click managed using onclick property')
}
```

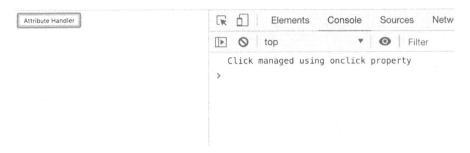

Figure 4-2. *Example of an onclick property handler*

I just stated that this is a quick and dirty solution. It's easy to grasp why it's quick, but why is it also *dirty*? Even if it works, this kind of solution is usually considered bad practice. The main reason is that you can attach just one handler at a time with properties. So if a piece of code overwrites your onclick handler, your original handler is lost forever. In the next section, you see another, better, approach: the addEventListener method.

Attach Handlers with addEventListener

Every DOM node that can handle events implements the EventTarget interface. The most important method of this interface is addEventListener, which is useful for adding event handlers to a DOM node. Listing 4-2 shows how to add a simple event handler to a button click using this technique.

Listing 4-2. Click Handler with addEventListener

```
const button = document.querySelector('button')
button.addEventListener('click', () => {
  console.log('Clicked using addEventListener')
})
```

The first parameter is the event type. In the last example, you manage the click, but you can add listeners to handle any supported event type. The second parameter is the callback that's invoked when the event is triggered.

In contrast to the property method, with addEventListener, you can attach all the handlers you need, as shown in Listing 4-3.

Listing 4-3. Multiple Click Event Handlers

```
const button = document.querySelector('button')
button.addEventListener('click', () => {
  console.log('First handler')
})
button.addEventListener('click', () => {
  console.log('Second handler')
})
```

Keep in mind that when an element is not present anymore in the DOM, you should remove its event listeners as well in order to prevent memory leaks. To do that, you can use the removeEventListener method, as shown in Listing 4-4.

Listing 4-4. Removing Event Handlers

```
const button = document.querySelector('button')
const firstHandler = () => {
  console.log('First handler')
}

const secondHandler = () => {
  console.log('Second handler')
}
```

```
button.addEventListener('click', firstHandler)
button.addEventListener('click', secondHandler)

window.setTimeout(() => {
  button.removeEventListener('click', firstHandler)
  button.removeEventListener('click', secondHandler)
  console.log('Removed Event Handlers')
}, 1000)
```

The most important thing to notice in the previous snippet is that, in order to remove an event handler, you should keep a reference to it to pass it as a parameter in the removeEventListener method.

The Event Object

In all the code that you have analyzed so far, event handlers were created without parameters. But the signature of an event handler can contain a parameter that represents the event emitted by the DOM node or the system. Listing 4-5 simply prints this event in the console.

As you can see in Figure 4-3, the event contains a lot of useful information, like the coordinates of the pointer, the type of event, the element that triggered the event, and so on.

Listing 4-5. Printing the Event Object to the Console

```
const button = document.querySelector('button')
button.addEventListener('click', e => {
  console.log('event', e)
})
```

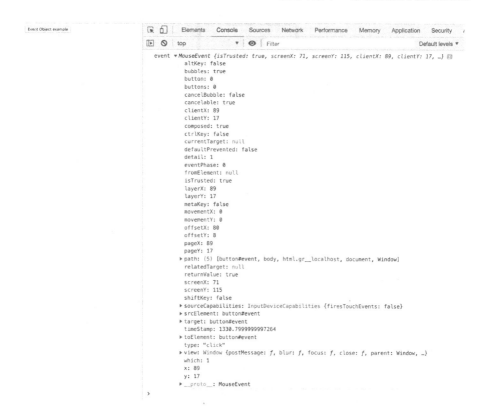

Figure 4-3. *Printing the event object to the console*

Any event dispatched in a web application implements the Event interface. Based on its type, the Event object can implement a more specific interface that extends Event. A click event (but also dblclick, mouseup, and mousedown) implements the MouseEvent interface. This interface contains information about the coordinates or the movement of the pointer during the event and other useful data. The MouseEvent interface hierarchy is shown in Figure 4-4.

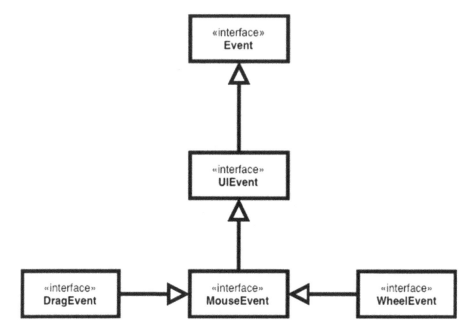

Figure 4-4. *MouseEvent interface hierarchy*

For a complete reference of Event and the other interfaces, you can read the MDN guide.[3]

The DOM Event Lifecycle

When you read some code that uses the addEventListener method to add a handler, you usually see something like this:

```
button.addEventListener('click', handler, false)
```

The third parameter is called useCapture, and its default value is false. This parameter has not always been optional. You should include it for the widest possible browser compatibility. But what does it mean

---

[3] https://developer.mozilla.org/en-US/docs/Web/API/Event

to capture an event? And what happens if you set the useCapture to true? I'll explain it with an example. Consider the HTML structure in Listing 4-6.

Listing 4-6. A Simple Nested HTML Structure

```
<body>
    <div>
        This is a container
        <button>Click Here</button>
    </div>
</body>
```

In Listing 4-7, event handlers are attached to both DOM elements—the div and the button.

Listing 4-7. Showing the Bubble Phase Mechanism

```
const button = document.querySelector('button')
const div = document.querySelector('div')

div.addEventListener('click', () => {
  console.log('Div Clicked')
}, false)

button.addEventListener('click', () => {
  console.log('Button Clicked')
}, false)
```

What happens if you click the button? Given that the button is inside the div, both handlers will be invoked, starting with the button one. So the event object starts from the DOM node that triggered it (in this case, button) and goes up to all its ancestors. This mechanism is called the "bubble phase" or event bubbling. You can stop the bubble chain with the stopPropagation method from the Event interface. In Listing 4-8, this method is used in the button handler to stop the div handler.

73

Listing 4-8. Stopping the Bubble Chain

```
const button = document.querySelector('button')
const div = document.querySelector('div')

div.addEventListener('click', () => {
  console.log('Div Clicked')
}, false)

button.addEventListener('click', e => {
  e.stopPropagation()
  console.log('Button Clicked')
}, false)
```

In this case, the div handler is not invoked. This technique could be useful when you have a complex layout, but if you rely often on the order of the handlers, your code could become very hard to maintain. In these cases, the event delegation pattern could be useful. I talk more about event delegation at the end of this chapter.

You can use the useCapture parameter to reverse the order of execution of the handlers. In Listing 4-9, the div handler is invoked before the button one, as shown in Figure 4-5.

Listing 4-9. Using useCapture to Reverse the Order of the Event Handlers

```
const button = document.querySelector('button')
const div = document.querySelector('div')

div.addEventListener('click', e => {
  console.log('Div Clicked')
}, true)

button.addEventListener('click', e => {
  console.log('Button Clicked')
}, true)
```

Figure 4-5. *Using the capture phase*

In other words, using `true` for the `useCapture` parameter during the invocation of `addEventListener` means that you want to add the event handler to the capture phase instead of the bubble phase. While in the bubble phase, the handlers use a bottom-up process; in the capture phase, it's the opposite. The system starts managing handlers from the `<html>` tag and goes deeper until the event's trigger element is managed. It's important to remember that browsers run the capture phase (top-down) and then the bubble phase (bottom-up) for every DOM event that is generated. The third phase, called the target phase, occurs when the event reaches the target element, in this case, the `button`. To summarize, this is the lifecycle of most of the DOM events:

1. Capture phase: From `html` to the target element.

2. Target phase: The event reaches the target element.

3. Bubble phase: From the target element to `html`.

A more detailed version of this lifecycle is visible in Figure 4-6.

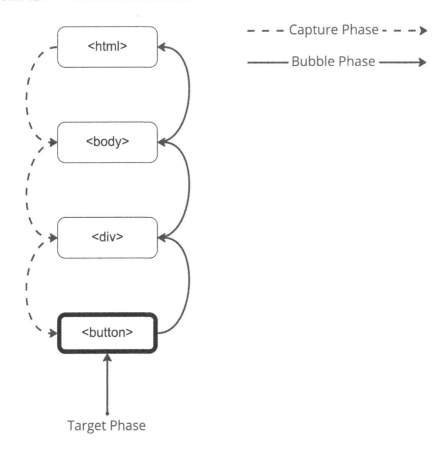

Figure 4-6. Event lifecycle

These phases exist for historical reasons. In the dark days, some browsers just managed the capture phase, and others managed only the bubble phase. Generally, using just bubble phase handlers is okay, but knowing about the capture phase is important for handling some complex situations.

Using Custom Events

The only event that you have handled so far is a button click. Similarly, you can handle many different kinds of events, like the one discussed at the beginning of the chapter. But the DOM Events API is far more *powerful*. You can define custom event types and handle them like any other event.

This is an essential part of the DOM Events API, because you can create DOM events bound to the *domain* based on what happened in the system. You can create an event handler for login or logout or something that happened to the dataset, such as creating a new record in a list.

As you can see in Listing 4-10, to create a custom event, you have to use the constructor function called CustomEvent.

Listing 4-10. Firing Custom Events

```
const EVENT_NAME = 'FiveCharInputValue'
const input = document.querySelector('input')

input.addEventListener('input', () => {
  const { length } = input.value
  console.log('input length', length)
  if (length === 5) {
    const time = (new Date()).getTime()
    const event = new CustomEvent(EVENT_NAME, {
      detail: {
        time
      }
    })

    input.dispatchEvent(event)
  }
})
```

```
input.addEventListener(EVENT_NAME, e => {
  console.log('handling custom event...', e.detail)
})
```

While managing the input event, you check for the length of
the value itself. If the length is exactly five, you fire a special event
called FiveCharInputValue. A standard event listener with the usual
addEventListener method handles the custom event. Notice how you
can use the same API for a standard event (input) and for a custom one.
You can also pass additional data to the handlers with the detail object
that you used in the constructor (in this case, a timestamp). The result of
Listing 4-10 is visible in Figure 4-7.

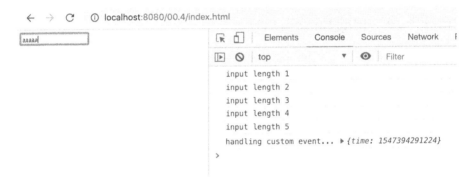

Figure 4-7. *Using custom events*

In the next chapter about web components, I show you how to use
custom events to let components communicate with each other.

Adding Events to TodoMVC

Now that you have learned the basic concepts of the DOM Events API, you
can add event handling to the TodoMVC application. Take another look at
a complete TodoMVC application (see Figure 4-8) in order to understand
which events need to be handled.

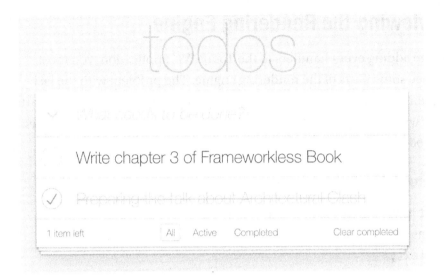

Figure 4-8. *The complete TodoMVC application*

The events that you need to manage are as follows:

- **Delete an item:** Click the cross to the right of every row.

- **Toggle a thing as complete or not:** Click the circle to the left of every row.

- **Change the filter:** Click the filter name at the bottom.

- **Create a new item:** Input a value in the top input box and press Enter on the keyboard.

- **Remove all completed items:** Click the Clear Completed label.

- **Toggle all items as completed or not:** Click the chevron in the top-left corner.

- **Edit an item:** Double-click the row, then change the value and press Enter on the keyboard.

Reviewing the Rendering Engine

Before adding event handlers to the TodoMVC application, you must change some parts of the rendering engine. The problem with the last implementation that you developed in the last chapter is that some parts work with strings instead of DOM elements. In Listing 4-11, you can see the todos component from the previous chapter.[4]

Listing 4-11. Todos Component

```
const getTodoElement = todo => {
  const {
    text,
    completed
  } = todo

  return `
      <li ${completed ? 'class="completed"' : ''}>
        <div class="view">
          <input
            ${completed ? 'checked' : ''}
            class="toggle"
            type="checkbox">
          <label>${text}</label>
          <button class="destroy"></button>
        </div>
        <input class="edit" value="${text}">
      </li>`
}
```

---

[4] You can find the complete code of this example on GitHub at https://github. com/Apress/Frameworkless-Front-End-Development-2nd-ed./tree/main/ Chapter03/05.

```
export default (targetElement, { todos }) => {
  const newTodoList = targetElement.cloneNode(true)
  const todosElements = todos
    .map(getTodoElement)
    .join('')
  newTodoList.innerHTML = todosElements
  return newTodoList
}
```

Every todo element in the list is created with a string, then joined together and then added to the parent list with innerHTML. But you cannot add event handlers to strings; you need DOM nodes to invoke addEventListener.

The Template Element

There are a bunch of different techniques to create DOM nodes programmatically. One of them is to use document.createElement, an API that lets developers create new empty DOM nodes. You can see an example in Listing 4-12.

Listing 4-12. document.createElement Examples

```
const newDiv = document.createElement('div')
if(!condition){
  newDiv.classList.add('disabled')
}

const newSpan = document.createElement('span')
newSpan.textContent = 'Hello World!'

newDiv.appendChild(newSpan)
```

You could use this API to create an empty li, and then add the various div, input, and so on. But such code will be tough to read and maintain. Another (better) option is to keep the markup of the todo element inside a template tag in the index.html file. A template tag is just what its name suggests: An invisible tag you can use as a "stamp" for your rendering engine. Listing 4-13 shows a template example of the todo item.

Listing 4-13. todo-item template Element

```
<template id="todo-item">
  <li>
    <div class="view">
      <input class="toggle" type="checkbox">
      <label></label>
      <button class="destroy"></button>
    </div>
    <input class="edit">
  </li>
</template>
```

In Listing 4-14, this template is used in the todos component as a "stamp" to create a new li DOM node.

Listing 4-14. Using the Template to Generate todo Items

```
let template

const createNewTodoNode = () => {
  if (!template) {
    template = document.getElementById('todo-item')
  }

  return template
    .content
```

82

```
      .firstElementChild
      .cloneNode(true)
}

const getTodoElement = todo => {
  const {
    text,
    completed
  } = todo

  const element = createNewTodoNode()

  element.querySelector('input.edit').value = text
  element.querySelector('label').textContent = text

  if (completed) {
    element
      .classList
      .add('completed')

    element
      .querySelector('input.toggle')
      .checked = true
  }

  return element
}

export default (targetElement, { todos }) => {
  const newTodoList = targetElement.cloneNode(true)

  newTodoList.innerHTML = ''

  todos
    .map(getTodoElement)
    .forEach(element => {
```

```
        newTodoList.appendChild(element)
    })

  return newTodoList
}
```

You can then extend the template technique to all the applications, thus creating an app component. The first step is to wrap all the markup of the todo list in a template element, as shown in Listing 4-15.

Listing 4-15. Using the Template for the Entire App

```
<body>
    <template id="todo-item">
        <!-- Put here todo item content-->
    </template>
    <template id="todo-app">
        <section class="todoapp">
            <!-- Put here app content-->
        </section>
    </template>
    <div id="root">
        <div data-component="app"></div>
    </div>
</body>
```

In Listing 4-16, a new component called app is created. This component utilizes the newly created template to generate its content. This is the last part of the template portion of the TodoMVC application. This new version of the application[5] will be the base of the event handlers architecture.

---

[5] The complete code of the application is hosted on GitHub at https://github. com/Apress/Frameworkless-Front-End-Development-2nd-ed./tree/main/ Chapter04/01.1.

Listing 4-16. App Component with Template

```
let template

const createAppElement = () => {
  if (!template) {
    template = document.getElementById('todo-app')
  }

  return template
    .content
    .firstElementChild
    .cloneNode(true)
}

export default (targetElement) => {
  const newApp = targetElement.cloneNode(true)
  newApp.innerHTML = ''
  newApp.appendChild(createAppElement())
  return newApp
}
```

A Basic Event-Handling Architecture

Now that you have a new rendering engine that works with DOM elements instead of strings, you can attach event handlers to the application. Let's start with a high-level overview and then with a working example. The rendering engine is based on pure functions that get a state and generate a DOM tree.

You also know that for every new state, you can generate a new DOM tree and apply a virtual DOM algorithm. In this scenario, you can easily inject the event handlers in this "loop." After every event, you will manipulate the state and invoke the main render function again with this new state. Figure 4-9 shows a schema of this *state-render-event* loop.

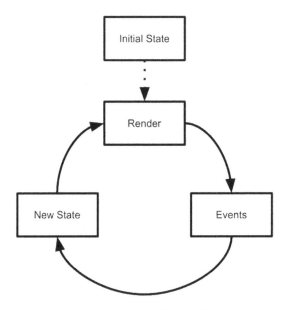

Figure 4-9. *High-level architecture of event handling*

You can test the *state-render-event* loop by just enumerating the steps of a simple use case for your application. Imagine a user who adds and deletes an item from the list:

- **Initial state:** Empty todo list

- **Render:** Show the user an empty list

- **Event:** The user creates a new item named "dummy item"

- **New state:** The todo list with one item

- **Render:** Show the user a list with one item

- **Event:** The user deletes the item

- **New State:** Empty todo list

- **Render:** Show the user an empty list

Now that you defined the high-level architecture, it's time to implement it. The code in Listing 4-17 illustrates these events and the related state modification in the controller.

Listing 4-17. A Controller with Events

```
const state = {
  todos: [],
  currentFilter: 'All'
}

const events = {
  deleteItem: (index) => {
    state.todos.splice(index, 1)
    render()
  },
  addItem: text => {
    state.todos.push({
      text,
      completed: false
    })
    render()
  }
}

const render = () => {
  window.requestAnimationFrame(() => {
    const main = document.querySelector('#root')

    const newMain = registry.renderRoot(
      main,
      state,
      events)
```

```
    applyDiff(document.body, main, newMain)
  })
}
```

```
render()
```

The entry point of the rendering engine, the `renderRoot` function, now takes a third parameter that contains the events. You will see in a moment that this new parameter is accessible to all your components. The events are straightforward functions that modify the state and manually invoke a new render. In a real-world application, I suggest creating some kind of "event registry" that helps developers quickly add handlers and automatically invoke a new render cycle. For now, this implementation is *good enough*.

In Listing 4-18, the `addItem` handler is used by the `app` component to add a new item to the list

Listing 4-18. App Component with addItem Event

```
let template

const getTemplate = () => {
  if (!template) {
    template = document.getElementById('todo-app')
  }

  return template.content.firstElementChild.cloneNode(true)
}

const addEvents = (targetElement, events) => {
  targetElement
    .querySelector('.new-todo')
    .addEventListener('keypress', e => {
      if (e.key === 'Enter') {
        events.addItem(e.target.value)
```

```
      e.target.value = ''
    }
  })
}
export default (targetElement, state, events) => {
  const newApp = targetElement.cloneNode(true)

  newApp.innerHTML = ''
  newApp.appendChild(getTemplate())

  addEvents(newApp, events)

  return newApp
}
```

For every render cycle, you generate a new DOM element and attach an event handler to the input used to insert the value of the new item. If the user presses Enter, the addItem function is fired, and the input is cleared. However, in the previous snippet, there is something that may seem out of place. You clear the value of the input inside the event itself. *Why is the input's value not part of the state like the list of todos or the current filter?* I address this topic in Chapter 8 about state management, so for now, just ignore this problem.

The other action that the user can do in this first example is delete an item. So, the component that needs access to events to achieve this goal is todos, as you can see in Listing 4-19.

Listing 4-19. The todos Component with Events

```
const getTodoElement = (todo, index, events) => {
  const {
    text,
    completed
  } = todo
```

```
const element = createNewTodoNode()

element.querySelector('input.edit').value = text
element.querySelector('label').textContent = text

if (completed) {
  element.classList.add('completed')
  element
    .querySelector('input.toggle')
    .checked = true
}

const handler = e => events.deleteItem(index)

element
  .querySelector('button.destroy')
  .addEventListener('click', handler)

return element
}

export default (targetElement, { todos }, events) => {
  const newTodoList = targetElement.cloneNode(true)

  newTodoList.innerHTML = ''

  todos
    .map((todo, index) => getTodoElement(todo, index, events))
    .forEach(element => {
      newTodoList.appendChild(element)
    })

  return newTodoList
}
```

This second example is very similar to the previous one, but this time I created a different handler for every todo item.[6]

Event Delegation

One of the features provided with most front-end frameworks, and one that is usually well hidden under the hood, is event delegation. To understand what event delegation is, let's continue with an example. Listing 4-20 contains a revised version of Listing 4-19 based on event delegation.

Listing 4-20. The todos Component with Event Delegation

```
const getTodoElement = (todo, index) => {
  const {
    text,
    completed
  } = todo

  const element = createNewTodoNode()

  element.querySelector('input.edit').value = text
  element.querySelector('label').textContent = text

  if (completed) {
    element.classList.add('completed')
    element
      .querySelector('input.toggle')
      .checked = true
  }
```

---

[6]You can read the code of the complete application with all the events on GitHub (https://github.com/Apress/Frameworkless-Front-End-Development-2nd-ed./tree/main/Chapter04/01.3).

91

```
  element
    .querySelector('button.destroy')
    .dataset
    .index = index

  return element
}

export default (targetElement, state, events) => {
  const { todos } = state
  const { deleteItem } = events
  const newTodoList = targetElement.cloneNode(true)

  newTodoList.innerHTML = ''

  todos
    .map((todo, index) => getTodoElement(todo, index))
    .forEach(element => {
      newTodoList.appendChild(element)
    })

  newTodoList.addEventListener('click', e => {
    if (e.target.matches('button.destroy')) {
      deleteItem(e.target.dataset.index)
    }
  })

  return newTodoList
}
```

The difference with the previous component is that you have just one event handler attached to the list itself and not a separate event handler for every row. This approach can improve performance and memory usage when you have a very long list.

Notice the usage of the matches API[7] to check if an element is the "real" event target. Using this approach on a larger scale, you can also achieve just one event handler on the body of the web page. Building an event delegation library is out of the scope of this book, but there are a bunch of libraries you can use in your projects. One of these libraries is gator.js,[8] and it's easy to use. Listing 4-21 shows a simple example of a handler attached using this library.

Listing 4-21. The gator.js Example

```
Gator(document).on('click', 'button.destroy', e => {
  deleteItem(e.target.dataset.index)
})
```

I want to give you the advice I used to close the last chapter. Don't add any optimization like event delegation until you need it. Remember the YAGNI principle and consider that adding an event delegation library like gator.js to an existing project can be done iteratively just for the most critical parts.

Summary

This chapter covered some basic concepts of the DOM Events API. You learned how to attach and remove event handlers, the difference between bubble and capture phases, and how to create custom events. Then, you updated the TodoMVC application, adding the events to add and remove an item.

---

[7] https://developer.mozilla.org/en-US/docs/Web/API/Element/matches
[8] https://craig.is/riding/gators

Finally, you learned about the concept of event delegation, an important pattern to keep your frameworkless applications performant enough for non-trivial contexts.

In the next chapter, you learn how to work effectively with web components, which are a standard way to create components in web applications.

CHAPTER 5

Web Components

All the major front-end frameworks that developers use today have *something* in common. They all use components as basic blocks for building the UI. Chapter 3 showed you how to create a component registry based on pure functions. On (almost) all modern browsers, it's possible to create components for your web applications with a set of *native* APIs. This suite of APIs is called Web Components.

The APIs

Web Components consist of three main technologies that let developers build and publish reusable UI components:

- **HTML templates**: The `<template>` tag is useful if you want to keep content that is not rendered but that can be used by JavaScript code as a "stamp" to create dynamic content.

- **Custom elements**: This API lets developers create their own fully-featured DOM elements.

© Francesco Strazzullo 2023
F. Strazzullo, *Frameworkless Front-End Development*,
https://doi.org/10.1007/978-1-4842-9351-5_5

- **Shadow DOM:**[1] This technique is useful if the Web Components should not be affected by the DOM outside the component itself. It's handy if you're creating a component library or a widget that you want to share with the world.

The Custom Elements API

The Custom Elements API is the core factor of the Web Components suite. In a nutshell, it permits you to create custom HTML tags like this one:

```
<app-calendar/>
```

It is no coincidence that I used the name `app-calendar`. When you create a custom tag with the Custom Elements API, you have to use at least two words separated by a dash. Every one-word tag is for the sole use of the World Wide Web Consortium (W3C). Listing 5-1 shows a `Hello World!` label, the simplest custom element possible.

Note   A custom element is just a JavaScript class that extends `HTMLElement`.

Listing 5-1. HelloWorld Custom Element

```
export default class HelloWorld extends HTMLElement {
  connectedCallback () {
    window.requestAnimationFrame(() => {
```

---

[1] Shadow DOM and Virtual DOM solve two completely different problems. Shadow DOM is about encapsulation, while Virtual DOM is about performances. For more information, I suggest reading this post: `https://developer.com/shadow-dom-virtual-dom-889bf78ce701`.

```
      this.innerHTML = '<div>Hello World!</div>'
    })
  }
}
```

connectedCallback is one of the lifecycle methods of a custom
element. This method is invoked when the component is attached to the
DOM. It's very similar to the componentDidMount method from React. It's a
good place to render the content of the component, such as to start timers
or to fetch data from the network. Similarly, the disconnectedCallback is
invoked when the component is removed from the DOM. This is a useful
method for any cleanup operation.

To actually use this newly created component, you need to add it to
the browser component registry. To achieve this goal, you need to use
the define method of the window.customElements property, as shown in
Listing 5-2.

Listing 5-2. Adding HelloWorld to Custom Elements Registry

```
import HelloWorld from './components/HelloWorld.js'

window
  .customElements
  .define('hello-world', HelloWorld)
```

To add a component to the browser component registry means to
connect a tag name—'hello-world' in this case—to a custom element
class. After that, you can simply use the component using the custom tag
that you created:

```
(<hello-world/>)
```

Managing Attributes

The most important feature of Web Components is that developers can make new components that are compatible with any framework out there. Not just with React or Angular, but with any web application out there, like some legacy application built with Java Server Pages or some other old tool. But, in order to achieve this goal, your components need to have the same public API of any other standard HTML element. So if you want to add an attribute to a custom element, you need to be sure that you can manage this attribute the same as any other attribute. For a standard element, like a <input>, you can set an attribute in three ways.

The first, and most intuitive, way is to add the attribute directly on the HTML markup.

```
<input type="text" value="Frameworkless">
```

On the JavaScript side, you can manipulate the value attribute with a setter.

```
input.value = 'Frameworkless'
```

Alternatively, it's possible to use the setAttribute method.

```
input.setAttribute('value', 'Frameworkless')
```

All these methods accomplish the same result: They change the value attribute of the input element. They are also synchronized. If you put the value via the markup, you will read the same value with the getter or the getAttribute method. In the same way, if you change the value with the setter or the setAttribute method, the markup will synchronize with the new attribute.

If you want to create an attribute for a custom element, you need to keep in mind this characteristic of HTML elements. Listing 5-3 adds a color attribute to the HelloWorld component, which you can use to change the color of the label.

Listing 5-3. HelloWorld with an Attribute

```
const DEFAULT_COLOR = 'black'

export default class HelloWorld extends HTMLElement {
  get color () {
    return this.getAttribute('color') || DEFAULT_COLOR
  }

  set color (value) {
    this.setAttribute('color', value)
  }

  connectedCallback () {
    window.requestAnimationFrame(() => {
      const div = document.createElement('div')
      div.textContent = 'Hello World!'

      div.style.color = this.color

      this.appendChild(div)
    })
  }
}
```

As you can see, the color getter/setter is just a wrapper around getAttribute/setAttribute. So, the three ways to set an attribute are automatically synchronized. To set the color of the component, you can use the setter (or setAttribute), or you can just set the color via markup. You can see an example of the color attribute in Listing 5-4, and the related result is shown in Figure 5-1.

99

Listing 5-4. Using the Color Attribute for the HelloWorld Component

```
<hello-world></hello-world>
<hello-world color="red"></hello-world>
<hello-world color="green"></hello-world>
```

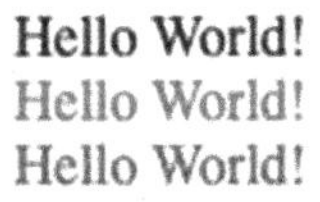

Hello World!
Hello World!
Hello World!

Figure 5-1. *The HelloWorld component*

When you use this approach when designing attributes for a Web Component, the component itself is very easy to release to other developers. You just need to release the code of the component in some kind of CDN, and then everyone can use it, without any specific instructions. You just defined an attribute in the same way the W3C did for standard components.

Nevertheless, this approach comes with a drawback: HTML attributes are strings. When you're in need of an attribute that is not a string, you need to convert the attribute before using it.

attributeChangedCallback

In Listing 5-4, you read the value of the `color` attribute in the `connectedCallback` method and apply that value to the DOM. But what happens if you change the attribute after the initial render with a simple click event handler, as shown in Listing 5-5?

Listing 5-5. Changing the Color of HelloWorld Component

```
const changeColorTo = color => {
  document
    .querySelectorAll('hello-world')
    .forEach(helloWorld => {
      helloWorld.color = color
    })
}

document
  .querySelector('button')
  .addEventListener('click', () => {
    changeColorTo('blue')
  })
```

When the button is clicked, the handler changes the color attribute of every HelloWorld component to blue. But on the screen, nothing happens. A quick and dirty way to solve this problem is to add some kind of DOM manipulation in the setter:

```
set color (value) {
  this.setAttribute('color', value)
  //Update DOM with the new color
}
```

But this approach is very fragile because if you use the setAttribute method instead of the color setter, the DOM will not be updated either. The right way to manage attributes that can change during the lifecycle of a component is to use the attributeChangedCallback method. This method (like its name suggests) is invoked every time some attributes change. You can modify the code of the HelloWorld component, like in Listing 5-6, to update the DOM every time a new color attribute is provided.

Listing 5-6. Updating the Color of the Label

```
const DEFAULT_COLOR = 'black'

export default class HelloWorld extends HTMLElement {
  static get observedAttributes () {
    return ['color']
  }

  get color () {
    return this.getAttribute('color') || DEFAULT_COLOR
  }

  set color (value) {
    this.setAttribute('color', value)
  }

  attributeChangedCallback (name, oldValue, newValue) {
    if (!this.div) {
      return
    }

    if (name === 'color') {
      this.div.style.color = newValue
    }
  }

  connectedCallback () {
    window.requestAnimationFrame(() => {
      this.div = document.createElement('div')
      this.div.textContent = 'Hello World!'
      this.div.style.color = this.color
      this.appendChild(this.div)
    })
  }
}
```

The `attributeChangedCallback` method accepts three parameters—the name of the attribute that is changed, the old value of the attribute, and the new value.

Note   Not every attribute will trigger `attributeChangedCallback`, only the attributes listed in the `observedAttributes` array.

Virtual DOM Integration

The Virtual DOM algorithm from Chapter 2 is completely pluggable into any custom element. Listing 5-7 shows a new version of the `HelloWorld` component that, every time that the color changes, invokes the Virtual DOM algorithm to modify the color of the label.[2]

Listing 5-7. Using Virtual DOM in a Custom Element

```
import applyDiff from './applyDiff.js'

const DEFAULT_COLOR = 'black'

const createDomElement = color => {
  const div = document.createElement('div')
  div.textContent = 'Hello World!'
  div.style.color = color
  return div
}

export default class HelloWorld extends HTMLElement {
  static get observedAttributes () {
    return ['color']
  }
```

---

[2] The complete code of this example is visible at `https://github.com/Apress/Frameworkless-Front-End-Development-2nd-ed./tree/main/Chapter05/00.3`.

```
get color () {
  return this.getAttribute('color') || DEFAULT_COLOR
}

set color (value) {
  this.setAttribute('color', value)
}

attributeChangedCallback (name, oldValue, newValue) {
  if (!this.hasChildNodes()) {
    return
  }

  applyDiff(
    this,
    this.firstElementChild,
    createDomElement(newValue)
  )
}

connectedCallback () {
  window.requestAnimationFrame(() => {
    this.appendChild(createDomElement(this.color))
  })
}
}
```

For this scenario, using a Virtual DOM is clearly over-engineering. But it can be useful when your component has a lot of attributes. In that case, the code would be much more readable.

Custom Events

For this next example, you will analyze a more complex component, called GitHubAvatar. The purpose of this component is to show the avatar of a GitHub user given their username. To use this component, you just need to set the user attribute.

```
<github-avatar user="francesco-strazzullo"></github-avatar>
```

When the component is connected to the DOM, it shows a "loading" placeholder. Then it uses the GitHub Rest APIs to fetch the avatar image URL. If the request succeeds, the avatar is shown; otherwise, an error placeholder is shown. Figure 5-2 explains how this component works.

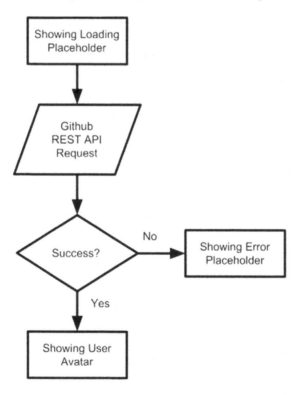

Figure 5-2. *Flowchart of the GitHubAvatar component*

You can look at the code of the GitHubAvatar component in Listing 5-8. For the sake of simplicity, I didn't manage changes in the user attribute with the attributeChangedCallback.

Listing 5-8. The GitHubAvatar Component

```
const ERROR_IMAGE = 'https://files-82ee7vgzc.now.sh'
const LOADING_IMAGE = 'https://files-8bga2nnt0.now.sh'

const getGitHubAvatarUrl = async user => {
  if (!user) {
    return
  }

  const url = `https://api.github.com/users/${user}`

  const response = await fetch(url)
  if (!response.ok) {
    throw new Error(response.statusText)
  }
  const data = await response.json()
  return data.avatar_url
}

export default class GitHubAvatar extends HTMLElement {
  constructor () {
    super()
    this.url = LOADING_IMAGE
  }

  get user () {
    return this.getAttribute('user')
  }
```

```
  set user (value) {
    this.setAttribute('user', value)
  }

  render () {
    window.requestAnimationFrame(() => {
      this.innerHTML = ''
      const img = document.createElement('img')
      img.src = this.url
      this.appendChild(img)
    })
  }

  async loadNewAvatar () {
    const { user } = this
    if (!user) {
      return
    }
    try {
      this.url = await getGitHubAvatarUrl(user)
    } catch (e) {
      this.url = ERROR_IMAGE
    }

    this.render()
  }

  connectedCallback () {
    this.render()
    this.loadNewAvatar()
  }
}
```

If you follow the previous flowchart, the code should be easy to read. To fetch the data from the GitHub API, the code uses `fetch`, a native way in modern browsers to make asynchronous HTTP requests. (You will learn more about this topic in the next chapter.) Figure 5-3 shows the result of various instances of the component.

Icons made by Eleonor Wang from www.flaticon.com is licensed by CC 3.0 BY
Icons made by Smashicons from www.flaticon.com is licensed by CC 3.0 BY

Figure 5-3. *The GitHubAvatar Example*

What if you want to react to the result of the HTTP request from the *outside* of the component itself? Remember that, when it's possible, a custom element should behave exactly like a standard DOM element. In the previous examples, you used attributes to pass information to a component, just like any other element. Following the same reasoning to get information from a component, you should use DOM events. Chapter 3 talked about the Custom Events API, which makes it possible to create DOM events that are bound to the domain and not to user interaction with the browser. Listing 5-9 shows a new version of the `GitHubAvatar` component that can emit two events—the first one when the avatar is loaded and the other one when an error occurs.

Listing 5-9. GitHubAvatar with Custom Events

```
const AVATAR_LOAD_COMPLETE = 'AVATAR_LOAD_COMPLETE'
const AVATAR_LOAD_ERROR = 'AVATAR_LOAD_ERROR'

export const EVENTS = {
  AVATAR_LOAD_COMPLETE,
  AVATAR_LOAD_ERROR
}
```

```
export default class GitHubAvatar extends HTMLElement {
  ...
  onLoadAvatarComplete () {
    const event = new CustomEvent(AVATAR_LOAD_COMPLETE, {
      detail: {
        avatar: this.url
      }
    })

    this.dispatchEvent(event)
  }

  onLoadAvatarError (error) {
    const event = new CustomEvent(AVATAR_LOAD_ERROR, {
      detail: {
        error
      }
    })

    this.dispatchEvent(event)
  }

  async loadNewAvatar () {
    const { user } = this
    if (!user) {
      return
    }
    try {
      this.url = await getGitHubAvatarUrl(user)
      this.onLoadAvatarComplete()
    } catch (e) {
      this.url = ERROR_IMAGE
      this.onLoadAvatarError(e)
    }
```

```
    this.render()
  }
  ...
}
```

Listing 5-10 attaches event handlers for the two kinds of events. In Figure 5-4, you can see that the right handlers are invoked.

Listing 5-10. Attaching Event Handlers to GitHubAvatar Events

```
import { EVENTS } from './components/GitHubAvatar.js'

document
  .querySelectorAll('github-avatar')
  .forEach(avatar => {
    avatar
      .addEventListener(
        EVENTS.AVATAR_LOAD_COMPLETE,
        e => {
          console.log(
            'Avatar Loaded',
            e.detail.avatar
          )
        })

    avatar
      .addEventListener(
        EVENTS.AVATAR_LOAD_ERROR,
        e => {
          console.log(
            'Avatar Loading error',
            e.detail.error
          )
        })
  })
```

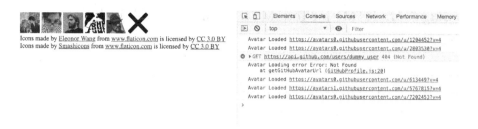

Figure 5-4. *GitHubAvatar with events*

Using Web Components for TodoMVC

It's time to build the usual TodoMVC application. This time you are going to use Web Components. Most of the code will be quite similar to the previous versions based on functions. I decided to split the application into three components—todomvc-app, todomvc-list, and todomvc-footer—as shown in Figure 5-5.

Figure 5-5. *TodoMVC components*

The first thing to analyze is the HTML part of the application. As you can see in Listing 5-11, this example uses the <template> element extensively.

Listing 5-11. HTML for TodoMVC Application with Web Components

```
<body>
    <template id="footer">
        <footer class="footer">
            <span class="todo-count">
            </span>
            <ul class="filters">
                <li>
                    <a href="#/">All</a>
                </li>
                <li>
                    <a href="#/active">Active</a>
                </li>
                <li>
                    <a href="#/completed">
                        Completed
                    </a>
                </li>
            </ul>
            <button class="clear-completed">
                Clear completed
            </button>
        </footer>
    </template>
    <template id="todo-item">
        <li>
            <div class="view">
                <input
```

```
                    class="toggle" type="checkbox">
                <label></label>
                <button class="destroy"></button>
            </div>
            <input class="edit">
        </li>
    </template>
    <template id="todo-app">
        <section class="todoapp">
            <header class="header">
                <h1>todos</h1>
                <input class="new-todo"
                  autofocus>
            </header>
            <section class="main">
                <input
                  id="toggle-all"
                  class="toggle-all"
                  type="checkbox">
                <label for="toggle-all">
                    Mark all as complete
                </label>
                <todomvc-list></todomvc-list>
            </section>
            <todomvc-footer></todomvc-footer>
        </section>
    </template>
    <todomvc-app></todomvc-app>
</body>
```

113

To keep the code simple, it only implements two of the many events that are present in the complete TodoMVC: adding an item and deleting it. This way, you can skip the code of the todomvc-footer and concentrate on todomvc-app and todomvc-list. (If you're interested, it's possible to check the complete code on GitHub.[3]) Let's start with the list in Listing 5-12.

Listing 5-12. TodoMVC List Web Component

```
const TEMPLATE = '<ul class="todo-list"></ul>'

export const EVENTS = {
  DELETE_ITEM: 'DELETE_ITEM'
}

export default class List extends HTMLElement {
  static get observedAttributes () {
    return [
      'todos'
    ]
  }

  get todos () {
    if (!this.hasAttribute('todos')) {
      return []
    }

    return JSON.parse(this.getAttribute('todos'))
  }

  set todos (value) {
    this.setAttribute('todos', JSON.stringify(value))
  }
```

---

[3] https://github.com/Apress/Frameworkless-Front-End-Development-2nd-ed./tree/main/Chapter05/01

```
  onDeleteClick (index) {
    const event = new CustomEvent(
      EVENTS.DELETE_ITEM,
      {
        detail: {
          index
        }
      }
  )

    this.dispatchEvent(event)
}

createNewTodoNode () {
    return this.itemTemplate
      .content
      .firstElementChild
      .cloneNode(true)
}

getTodoElement (todo, index) {
  const {
    text,
    completed
  } = todo

  const element = this.createNewTodoNode()

  element.querySelector('input.edit').value = text
  element.querySelector('label').textContent = text

  if (completed) {
    element.classList.add('completed')
    element
```

```
      .querySelector('input.toggle')
      .checked = true
  }

  element
    .querySelector('button.destroy')
    .dataset
    .index = index

  return element
}
updateList () {
  this.list.innerHTML = ''

  this.todos
    .map(this.getTodoElement)
    .forEach(element => {
      this.list.appendChild(element)
    })
  }

  connectedCallback () {
    this.innerHTML = TEMPLATE
    this.itemTemplate = document
      .getElementById('todo-item')

    this.list = this.querySelector('ul')

    this.list.addEventListener('click', e => {
      if (e.target.matches('button.destroy')) {
        this.onDeleteClick(e.target.dataset.index)
      }
    })
```

```
    this.updateList()
  }

  attributeChangedCallback () {
    this.updateList()
  }
}
```

Most of this code is similar to the code in the previous chapter. One of the differences is that you use a custom event to tell the outer world what is happening when the user clicks the Destroy button. The only attribute that this component accepts as input is the list of todo items. Every time that attribute changes, the list is rendered again. As you saw earlier in this chapter, it's quite easy to attach a Virtual DOM mechanism here.

Let's continue with the code of the todomvc-app component in Listing 5-13.

Listing 5-13. TodoMVC Application Components

```
import { EVENTS } from './List.js'

export default class App extends HTMLElement {
  constructor () {
    super()
    this.state = {
      todos: [],
      filter: 'All'
    }

    this.template = document
      .getElementById('todo-app')
  }
```

```
deleteItem (index) {
  this.state.todos.splice(index, 1)
  this.syncAttributes()
}

addItem (text) {
  this.state.todos.push({
    text,
    completed: false
  })
  this.syncAttributes()
}

syncAttributes () {
  this.list.todos = this.state.todos
  this.footer.todos = this.state.todos
  this.footer.filter = this.state.filter
}

connectedCallback () {
  window.requestAnimationFrame(() => {
    const content = this.template
      .content
      .firstElementChild
      .cloneNode(true)

    this.appendChild(content)

    this
      .querySelector('.new-todo')
      .addEventListener('keypress', e => {
        if (e.key === 'Enter') {
          this.addItem(e.target.value)
```

```
        e.target.value = ''
      }
    })

  this.footer = this
    .querySelector('todomvc-footer')

  this.list = this.querySelector('todomvc-list')
  this.list.addEventListener(
    EVENTS.DELETE_ITEM,
    e => {
      this.deleteItem(e.detail.index)
    }
  )

  this.syncAttributes()
  })
 }
}
```

This component has no attributes. It has an internal state instead.
Events from the DOM (standard or custom) change this state, and then
the component syncs its state with the attributes of its children in the
syncAttributes method. You will learn more about which components
should have an internal state in Chapter 8.

Web Components vs Rendering Functions

Now that you have seen Web Components in action, you can compare
them with the rendering functions approach that was analyzed in
Chapters 2 and 3. First consider some pros and cons of these two ways to
render DOM elements.

Code Style

To create a Web Component means to extend an HTMLElement, so it requires working with classes. If you're a functional programming enthusiast, you may feel some kind of itch working this way. On the other hand, if you're familiar with languages based on classes like Java or C# you may feel more confident with Web Components instead of functions.

There is no real winner here; it's really up to what you like most. As you saw in the last TodoMVC implementation you can take your rendering functions and wrap them with Web Components over time, so you can adapt your design to your scenario. For example, you can start with simple rendering functions and then wrap them in a Web Component if you need to release them in some kind of library.

Testability

This is an easy win for the rendering functions. To easily test rendering functions or custom elements, you just need a test runner like Jest[4] integrated into JSDom. In any case, rendering functions are easier to test because they have less overhead: They are just plain old JavaScript functions.

Portability

Web Components exist to be portable. The fact that they act exactly as any other DOM element is a killer feature if you need to use the same component in more applications. Later in the book, you learn how portability is a key factor when refactoring legacy projects.

---

[4]https://jestjs.io

Community

Component classes are a standard way to create DOM UI elements in most frameworks out there. This is a very useful thing to keep in mind if you have a large team or a team that needs to grow quickly. The more similar your code is to what people usually see, the more your code is readable.

Disappearing Frameworks

A very interesting side effect of the emergence of Web Component is the birth of a bunch of tools that are called *disappearing* (or *invisible*) *frameworks*. The basic idea is to write code with any other UI framework like React. Later, when you create the production bundle, the output will be just standard Web Components. In other words, during "compile time," the framework will just dissolve. The two most famous disappearing frameworks are Svelte[5] and Stencil.js.[6]

Stencil.js is based on TypeScript and JSX, and at first, it seems a strange mix between Angular and React. I consider Stencil.js particularly interesting because it's the tool that the team behind Ionic[7] built to create a new version of the famous mobile UI Kit entirely based on Web Components. Listing 5-14 shows how to build a simple Stencil.js component.

Listing 5-14. A Simple Stencil.js Component

```
import { Component, Prop } from '@stencil/core'

@Component({
  tag: 'hello-world'
```

---

[5] https://svelte.technology
[6] https://stenciljs.com
[7] https://ionicframework.com

```
})
export class HelloWorld {

  @Prop() name: string

  render() {
    return (
      <p>
        Hello {this.name}!
      </p>
    )
  }
}
```

Once this code is compiled, you can use this component like any other custom element.

```
<hello-world name="Francesco"></hello-world>
```

Summary

In this chapter, you learned about the main APIs behind the Web Component standard. You explored the main API of the suite, the Custom Elements API. You then built a new version of the TodoMVC application based on Web Components and evaluated the differences between this approach and rendering functions. At last, you learned what a "disappearing framework" is and how to create a very simple component with Stencil.js.

The next chapter focuses on building a frameworkless HTTP client to make asynchronous requests.

CHAPTER 6

HTTP Requests

In the previous chapters, you learned to render DOM elements and to react to events from systems or users, but a front-end application feeds on asynchronous data from a server. This chapter aims to show you how to build an HTTP client in a frameworkless way.

A Bit of History: The Birth of AJAX

Before the late 1990s, a complete page reload was required for every user action that needed any kind of data from the server. For people approaching web development (or web in general), today we use what we call *server-side rendering*. Starting in 1999, a group of applications—including Outlook, Gmail, and Google Maps—began to use a new technique: Loading data from the server after the initial page load without completely reloading the page. In 2005, Jesse James Garrett's famous blog post[1] named this technique AJAX, an acronym for "Asynchronous JavaScript and XML."

The central part of any AJAX application is the XMLHttpRequest object. As you will see later in this chapter, with this object, you can fetch data from the server with an HTTP request. The World Wide Web Consortium made the first specification draft for this object in 2006.

---

[1] `https://adaptivepath.org/ideas/ajax-new-approach-web-applications/`

© Francesco Strazzullo 2023
F. Strazzullo, *Frameworkless Front-End Development*,
https://doi.org/10.1007/978-1-4842-9351-5_6

As you just read, the "X" in AJAX stands for XML. When AJAX came out, web applications received data in XML from the server. Today, however, the more friendly (for JavaScript applications) JSON format is used. See Figure 6-1.

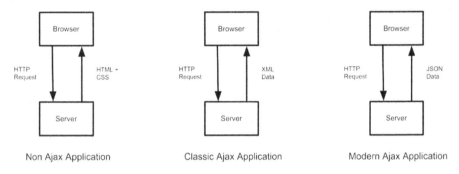

Figure 6-1. *Ajax vs non-Ajax architecture*

A To-Do List REST Server

To test the clients you will develop, you need a server from which you can fetch data. Listing 6-1 shows a straightforward REST server for Node.js with express,[2] a simple library[3] that quickly creates REST servers. This dummy server uses a temporary array to store the data related to the to-do list instead of a real database. To generate fake IDs, the program uses a small npm package called uuid[4] that lets developers generate UUIDs.

---

[2] https://expressjs.com/

[3] There are a lot of alternatives to express, like fastify (https://www.fastify.io/) or — if you prefer to build lambda functions — Claudia.js (https://claudiajs.com/) or serverless frameworks (https://www.serverless.com/).

[4] https://www.npmjs.com/package/uuid

Listing 6-1. A Dummy REST Server for Node.js

```
const app = express()
let todos = []

app.use(express.static('public'))
app.use(bodyParser.json())

app.get('/api/todos', (req, res) => {
  res.send(todos)
})

app.post('/api/todos', (req, res) => {
  const newTodo = {
    completed: false,
    ...req.body,
    id: uuidv4()
  }

  todos.push(newTodo)

  res.status(201)
  res.send(newTodo)
})

app.patch('/api/todos/:id', (req, res) => {
  const indexToUpdate = todos.findIndex(
    t => t.id === req.params.id
  )
  const oldTodo = todos[indexToUpdate]

  const newTodo = {
    ...oldTodo,
    ...req.body
  }
```

```
  todos[indexToUpdate] = newTodo

  res.send(newTodo)
})

app.put('/api/todos/:id', (req, res) => {
  const indexToUpdate = todos.findIndex(
    t => t.id === req.params.id
  )

  todos[indexToUpdate] = req.body

  res.send(req.body)
})

app.delete('/api/todos/:id', (req, res) => {
  todos = todos.filter(
    t => t.id !== req.params.id
  )

  res.status(204)
  res.send()
})

app.listen(PORT)
```

Representational State Transfer (REST)

This section explains the meaning of REST, the architecture behind the dummy server you just saw. If you already know the meaning of REST, you can skip this section.

REST is an acronym for *Representational State Transfer*, and it's a way to design and develop web services. The main abstraction of any REST API are the *resources*. You need to split your domain into resources; every resource should be read or manipulated, accessing specific URIs (Uniform Resource Identifiers). For example, to read the list of the users of your domain, you use the `https://api.example.com/users/` URI. To read the data of a specific user, the URI should have this form—`https://api.example.com/users/id1`—where `id1` is the ID of the user you want to read.

To manipulate (add, remove, or update) users, the same URIs are used, but with different HTTP verbs. Table 6-1 contains some examples of REST APIs for manipulating a list of users.

Table 6-1. *REST API Cheat Sheet*

Action	URI	HTTP Verb
Read all users	`https://api.example.com/users/`	GET
Read the data of the user with ID 1	`https://api.example.com/users/1`	GET
Create a new user	`https://api.example.com/users/`	POST
Replace the data of the user with ID 1	`https://api.example.com/users/1`	PUT
Update the data of the user with ID 1	`https://api.example.com/users/1`	PATCH
Delete the user with ID 1	`https://api.example.com/users/1`	DELETE

The actions listed in this table are quite straightforward. The only topic that may need an explanation is the difference between "update the data" (with PATCH) and "replace the data" (with PUT). When you use the verb PUT, you must pass in the body of the HTTP requests to the new user, complete in all its parts. On the other hand, when PATCH is used, the body should contain only the differences from the previous state. Note that, in the server in the previous paragraph, the newTodo object is merging the old to-do with the request body.[5]

Code Examples

In this section, you see how to create two different HTTP clients based on two different browser APIs—XMLHttpRequest and Fetch.

The Basic Structure

To show how HTTP clients work, I always use the same simple application shown in Figure 6-2. To keep the focus on the HTTP client, I do not use the TodoMVC application, but a simpler application with some buttons that execute the HTTP requests and print the results on-screen.[6]

Read Todos list   Add Todo   Update todo   [Delete Todo]

LIST TODOS: [] (11:52:35 GMT+0100 (Central European Standard Time))

ADD TODO: {"completed":false,"text":"A simple todo Element","id":"b4f21d42-1cb2-4b6a-bb4e-c13964cefa1e"} (11:52:36 GMT+0100 (Central European Standard Time))

LIST TODOS: [{"completed":false,"text":"A simple todo Element","id":"b4f21d42-1cb2-4b6a-bb4e-c13964cefa1e"}] (11:52:37 GMT+0100 (Central European Standard Time))

UPDATE TODO: {"completed":true,"text":"A simple todo Element","id":"b4f21d42-1cb2-4b6a-bb4e-c13964cefa1e"} (11:52:37 GMT+0100 (Central European Standard Time))

LIST TODOS: [{"completed":true,"text":"A simple todo Element","id":"b4f21d42-1cb2-4b6a-bb4e-c13964cefa1e"}] (11:52:38 GMT+0100 (Central European Standard Time))

DELETE TODO: undefined (11:52:39 GMT+0100 (Central European Standard Time))

Figure 6-2. *The application used to test the HTTP clients*

In Listing 6-2, you can see the index.html file of this application, while Listing 6-3 shows the main controller.

---

[5] To deepen the REST API topic, I suggest reading *RESTful Web APIs: Services for a Changing World* by Leonard Richardson and Mike Amundsen (www.amazon.com/gp/product/1449358063).

[6] The code of this application (and of the other implementations) is available at https://github.com/Apress/Frameworkless-Front-End-Development-2nd-ed./tree/main/Chapter06.

Listing 6-2. HTML for the HTTP Client Application

```html
<html>

<body>
    <button data-list>Read Todos list</button>
    <button data-add>Add Todo</button>
    <button data-update>Update todo</button>
    <button data-delete>Delete Todo</button>
    <div></div>
</body>

</html>
```

Listing 6-3. Main Controller for the HTTP Client Application

```javascript
import todos from './todos.js'

const NEW_TODO_TEXT = 'A simple todo Element'

const printResult = (action, result) => {
  const time = (new Date()).toTimeString()
  const node = document.createElement('p')
  node.textContent = '${action.toUpperCase()}: ${JSON.
  stringify(result)} (${time})'

  document
    .querySelector('div')
    .appendChild(node)
}

const onListClick = async () => {
  const result = await todos.list()
  printResult('list todos', result)
}
```

```
const onAddClick = async () => {
  const result = await todos.create(NEW_TODO_TEXT)
  printResult('add todo', result)
}

const onUpdateClick = async () => {
  const list = await todos.list()

  const { id } = list[0]
  const newTodo = {
    id,
    completed: true
  }

  const result = await todos.update(newTodo)
  printResult('update todo', result)
}

const onDeleteClick = async () => {
  const list = await todos.list()
  const { id } = list[0]

  const result = await todos.delete(id)
  printResult('delete todo', result)
}

document
  .querySelector('button[data-list]')
  .addEventListener('click', onListClick)

document
  .querySelector('button[data-add]')
  .addEventListener('click', onAddClick)
```

```
document
  .querySelector('button[data-update]')
  .addEventListener('click', onUpdateClick)

document
  .querySelector('button[data-delete]')
  .addEventListener('click', onDeleteClick)
```

This controller does not use the HTTP client directly. Instead, the HTTP request is wrapped in a todos API object. This kind of encapsulation is useful for many reasons. One of these reasons is testability: Replacing the todos object with a mock object that returns a static set of data (also called a *fixture*) is possible. This way, you can test your controller in isolation. Another reason is readability: Using model objects makes your code more explicit.

Tip   Never use bare HTTP clients in controllers. Try to encapsulate these functions in API objects.

Listing 6-4 shows the todos model object.

Listing 6-4. The todos Model Object

```
import http from './http.js'

const HEADERS = {
  'Content-Type': 'application/json'
}

const BASE_URL = '/api/todos'

const list = () => http.get(BASE_URL)
```

```
const create = text => {
  const todo = {
    text,
    completed: false
  }

  return http.post(
    BASE_URL,
    todo,
    HEADERS
  )
}

const update = newTodo => {
  const url = '${BASE_URL}/${newTodo.id}'
  return http.patch(
    url,
    newTodo,
    HEADERS
  )
}

const deleteTodo = id => {
  const url = '${BASE_URL}/${id}'
  return http.delete(
    url,
    HEADERS
  )
}
```

```
export default {
  list,
  create,
  update,
  delete: deleteTodo
}
```

The signature of the HTTP client is `http[verb](url, config)` for verbs that don't need a body, like `GET` or `DELETE`. For the other verbs, you can add the request body as a parameter with this signature: `http[verb](url, body, config)`.

Another way to build this kind of REST client is to use `http` as a function and not as an object, adding the verb as a parameter: `http(url, verb, body, config)`. Whatever you decide, try to keep it consistent.

Now that you understand the public contract of an HTTP client, it's time to look at the implementations.

XMLHttpRequest

The implementation in Listing 6-5 is based on `XMLHttpRequest`,[7] W3C's first attempt at creating a standard way to make asynchronous HTTP requests.

Listing 6-5. An HTTP client with XMLHttpRequest

```
const setHeaders = (xhr, headers) => {
  Object.entries(headers).forEach(entry => {
    const [
      name,
      value
    ] = entry
```

---

[7]https://developer.mozilla.org/en-US/docs/Web/API/XMLHttpRequest/Using_XMLHttpRequest

133

```
    xhr.setRequestHeader(
      name,
      value
    )
  })
}

const parseResponse = xhr => {
  const {
    status,
    responseText
  } = xhr

  let data
  if (status !== 204) {
    data = JSON.parse(responseText)
  }

  return {
    status,
    data
  }
}

const request = params => {
  return new Promise((resolve, reject) => {
    const xhr = new XMLHttpRequest()

    const {
      method = 'GET',
      url,
      headers = {},
      body
    } = params
```

```
    xhr.open(method, url)

    setHeaders(xhr, headers)

    xhr.send(JSON.stringify(body))

    xhr.onerror = () => {
      reject(new Error('HTTP Error'))
    }

    xhr.ontimeout = () => {
      reject(new Error('Timeout Error'))
    }

    xhr.onload = () => resolve(parseResponse(xhr))
  })
}

const get = async (url, headers) => {
  const response = await request({
    url,
    headers,
    method: 'GET'
  })

  return response.data
}

const post = async (url, body, headers) => {
  const response = await request({
    url,
    headers,
    method: 'POST',
    body
  })
```

```
  return response.data
}

const put = async (url, body, headers) => {
  const response = await request({
    url,
    headers,
    method: 'PUT',
    body
  })
  return response.data
}

const patch = async (url, body, headers) => {
  const response = await request({
    url,
    headers,
    method: 'PATCH',
    body
  })
  return response.data
}

const deleteRequest = async (url, headers) => {
  const response = await request({
    url,
    headers,
    method: 'DELETE'
  })
  return response.data
}
```

```
export default {
  get,
  post,
  put,
  patch,
  delete: deleteRequest
}
```

The core part of the HTTP client is the request method.
XMLHttpRequest is an API defined in 2006, so it's based on callbacks. You have the onload callback for a completed request, the onerror callback for any HTTP that ends with an error, and the ontimeout callback if the request times out. There is no timeout by default, but you can create one by modifying the timeout property of the xhr object.

The public API of the HTTP client is based on promises.[8] So the request method encloses the standard XMLHttpRequest request with a new promise. The public methods get, post, put, patch, and delete are just wrappers around the request method (passing the appropriate parameters) to make the code more readable.

This is the flow of an HTTP request with XMLHttpRequest, also visible in Figure 6-3:

1. Create a new XMLHttpRequest object (new XMLHttpRequest()).

2. Initialize the request to a specific URL (xhr.open(method, url)).

3. Configure the request (setting headers, timeout, and so on).

---

[8] https://developer.mozilla.org/en-US/docs/Web/JavaScript/Reference/Global_Objects/Promise

4. Send the request (`xhr.send(JSON.`
    `stringify(body))`),

5. Wait for the end of the request:

    a. If the request ends successfully, invoke the
        `onload` callback.

    b. If the request ends with an error, invoke the
        `onerror` callback.

    c. If the request times out, invoke the `ontimeout`
        callback.

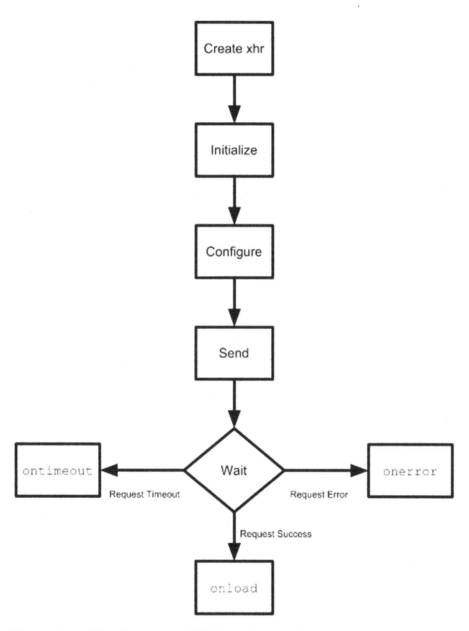

Figure 6-3. *The flow of an HTTP request with XMLHttpRequest*

Fetch

Fetch is an API created for accessing remote resources. Its purpose is to provide a standard definition of many network objects, like Request or Response.

In this way, these objects are interoperable with other APIs like ServiceWorker[9] and Cache.[10] In order to create a request, you need to use the window.fetch method, as you can see in the implementation of the HTTP client made with the Fetch API shown in Listing 6-6.

Listing 6-6. HTTP Client Based on the Fetch API

```
const parseResponse = async response => {
  const { status } = response
  let data
  if (status !== 204) {
    data = await response.json()
  }

  return {
    status,
    data
  }
}

const request = async params => {
  const {
    method = 'GET',
    url,
    headers = {},
```

---

[9]https://developer.mozilla.org/en-US/docs/Web/API/ServiceWorker
[10]https://developer.mozilla.org/en-US/docs/Web/API/Cache

```
    body
  } = params

  const config = {
    method,
    headers: new window.Headers(headers)
  }

  if (body) {
    config.body = JSON.stringify(body)
  }

  const response = await window.fetch(url, config)

  return parseResponse(response)
}

const get = async (url, headers) => {
  const response = await request({
    url,
    headers,
    method: 'GET'
  })

  return response.data
}

const post = async (url, body, headers) => {
  const response = await request({
    url,
    headers,
    method: 'POST',
    body
  })
  return response.data
}
```

```
const put = async (url, body, headers) => {
  const response = await request({
    url,
    headers,
    method: 'PUT',
    body
  })
  return response.data
}

const patch = async (url, body, headers) => {
  const response = await request({
    url,
    headers,
    method: 'PATCH',
    body
  })
  return response.data
}

const deleteRequest = async (url, headers) => {
  const response = await request({
    url,
    headers,
    method: 'DELETE'
  })
  return response.data
}

export default {
  get,
  post,
  put,
```

```
patch,
delete: deleteRequest
}
```

This HTTP client has the same public API as the one built with `XMLHttpRequest`: A `request` function is wrapped in a method for each HTTP verb that you want to use. The code of this second client is much more readable because `window.fetch` returns a promise, so you don't need a lot of boilerplate code to transform the classic callback-based approach of `XMLHttpRequest` into a more modern promise-based one.

The promise returned by `window.fetch` resolves a `Response` object. You can use this object to extract the body of the response sent by the server. Depending on the format of the data received, there are different methods available—for example, `text()`, `blob()`, and `json()`. In this scenario, you always have JSON data, so it's safe to use `json()`. Nevertheless, in a real-world application, you should use the right method according to the `Content-Type` header. You can read the complete reference of all the objects of the Fetch API on the Mozilla Developer Network (`https://developer.mozilla.org/en-US/docs/Web/API/Fetch_API/Using_Fetch`).

Reviewing the Architecture

Before continuing, let's review the architecture. The three different clients have the same public API. This characteristic of the architecture lets you change the library used for the HTTP requests (`XMLHttpRequest` or Fetch) with minimal effort. JavaScript is a dynamically-typed language, but you can think that all clients implement the `HTTPClient` interface. Figure 6-4 shows a UML diagram representing the relationship between the three implementations.

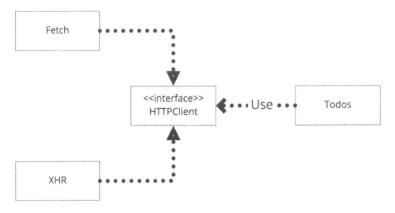

Figure 6-4. *UML diagram of the HTTP client*

To build a REST client, you must apply one of the most important principles of software design:

Program to an interface, not an implementation.

—Gang of Four

This principle, found in the book *Design Patterns: Elements of Reusable Object-Oriented Software* by the Gang of Four,[11] is very important when working with libraries.

Imagine having an extensive application with dozens of model objects needing network resources. If, in these objects, you use XMLHttpRequest directly, without using an HTTP client, changing the implementation to the Fetch API would be a costly (and tedious) task to accomplish. Using XMLHttpRequest in your model objects means programming to an implementation (the library) and not an interface (the HTTPClient).

---

[11] https://www.amazon.com/Design-Patterns-Object-Oriented-Addison-Wesley-Professional-ebook/dp/B000SEIBB8

Caution   When using a library, always create an interface around it. Changing the library to a new one will be easier if you need to.

Summary

In this chapter, you learned about the rise of AJAX and how it changed web development. Then you looked at two distinct ways to implement an HTTP client—based on XMLHttpRequest and based on the Fetch API.

The next chapter explains how to create a frameworkless routing system, an essential element of every SPA.

CHAPTER 7

Routing

The last chapter discussed AJAX and how it changed web development forever. Another essential technique that drastically changed how users interact with web applications are Single Page Applications (SPAs).

In this chapter, you will learn what an SPA is and how to build one of the core features of SPAs: a client-side routing system.

Single Page Applications

A single page application (SPA), as its name implies, is a web application that runs inside a single HTML page. When the user navigates from one view to another, the application dynamically repaints the view, giving the illusion of standard web navigation. This approach removes the delay that users can experience when navigating between pages in a standard multi-page application, thereby providing a better user experience.

This kind of application relies on AJAX to interact with the server. Nevertheless, not every AJAX application has to be an SPA. You can see the difference between a standard web application, a simple AJAX application, and a single page application in Figure 7-1.

© Francesco Strazzullo 2023
F. Strazzullo, *Frameworkless Front-End Development*,
https://doi.org/10.1007/978-1-4842-9351-5_7

Standard Web Application

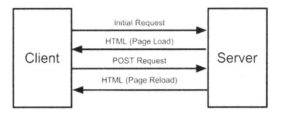

AJAX Web Application

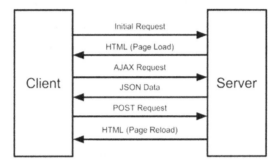

Single-page Application

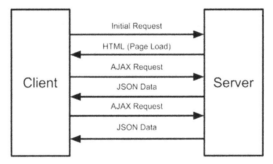

Figure 7-1. *A comparison of the web application architectures*

As explained in Chapter 2, frameworks like AngularJS and Ember contributed to making SPAs a mainstream approach when building web applications. These frameworks have an out-of-the-box system that defines routes via a routing system. From an architectural point of view (see Figure 7-2), every routing system has at least two core elements. The first one is a registry that collects the list of the routes of the application. In its simplest form, a route is an object that maps an URL to a DOM component. The other important part is having listeners on the current URL. When the URL changes, the router swaps the content of the body (or the main container) with the component bound to the route that matches the current URL.

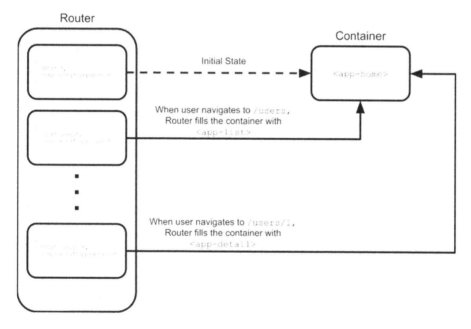

Figure 7-2. *High-level architecture of a routing system*

Code Examples

As in the last chapter, you will create three different versions of a routing system. You will begin with two frameworkless approaches, the first one based on fragment identifiers and the other one based on the History API. In the final one, you will use an open-source library called Navigo.[1]

Fragment Identifiers

Every URL can contain an optional part introduced by a hash, called a *fragment identifier*. Its purpose is to identify a specific section of a web page. For example, in the http://www.domain.org/foo.html#bar URL, the fragment identifier is bar and it identifies the HTML element with id="bar".

When navigating an URL that contains a fragment identifier, browsers will scroll the page until the element identified by the fragment is at the top of the viewport. You will use fragment identifiers to implement your first router object. This exercise starts with a simple example and makes it more complete in an iterative way.

A First Example

In this first example, you will build a very simple SPA with some links and a main container. In Listing 7-1, you can see the HTML template of this application.

Listing 7-1. The Basic SPA Template

```
<body>
    <header>
        <a href="#/">Go To Index</a>
```

---

[1] All the code examples are available at https://github.com/Apress/
Frameworkless-Front-End-Development-2nd-ed./tree/main/Chapter07.

```
        <a href="#/list">Go To List</a>
        <a href="#/dummy">Dummy Page</a>
    </header>
    <main>
    </main>
</body>
```

Using the anchors in the header, this URL will change to http://
localhost:8080/ to http://localhost:8080/#list and so on. When the
URL changes, the code will inject the current component inside the main
container. In this simple use case, the components are just plain functions
that update the contents of a DOM element, as you can see in Listing 7-2.

Listing 7-2. Basic SPA Components

```
export default container => {
  const home = () => {
    container
      .textContent = 'This is Home page'
  }

  const list = () => {
    container
      .textContent = 'This is List Page'
  }

  return {
    home,
    list
  }
}
```

When you're defining routes, it's a good practice to define a "not found" component to show when the URL doesn't match any component. This component (shown in Listing 7-3) should have the same structure as every other component.

Listing 7-3. The "Not Found" Component

```
const notFound = () => {
  container
    .textContent = 'Page Not Found!'
}
```

To make the router work, you need to configure it, linking the component to the right fragment. You can see how to configure the router in Listing 7-4.

Listing 7-4. Configuring a Basic Router

```
import createRouter from './router.js'
import createPages from './pages.js'

const container = document.querySelector('main')

const pages = createPages(container)

const router = createRouter()

router
  .addRoute('#/', pages.home)
  .addRoute('#/list', pages.list)
  .setNotFound(pages.notFound)
  .start()
```

The router has three public methods. The first one is addRoute, which defines a new route, a configuration object formed by the fragment, and the component. With the setNotFound method, you can set a generic component for any fragment that is not present in the registry. Finally, the start method initializes the router, starting to listen for URL changes.

Now that you analyzed the public interface of the router, it's time to take a look at the implementation in Listing 7-5.

Listing 7-5. Basic Router Implementation

```
export default () => {
  const routes = []
  let notFound = () => {}

  const router = {}

  const checkRoutes = () => {
    const currentRoute = routes.find(route => {
      return route.fragment === window.location.hash
    })

    if (!currentRoute) {
      notFound()
      return
    }

    currentRoute.component()
  }

  router.addRoute = (fragment, component) => {
    routes.push({
      fragment,
      component
    })

    return router
  }
```

```
router.setNotFound = cb => {
  notFound = cb
  return router
}

router.start = () => {
  window
    .addEventListener('hashchange', checkRoutes)

  if (!window.location.hash) {
    window.location.hash = '#/'
  }

  checkRoutes()
}

return router
}
```

As you can see, the current fragment identifier is stored in the hash property of the location object. There's also a very handy hashchange event that you can use to be notified every time the current fragment changes.

The core method of the router is checkRoutes. It looks for the route that matches the current fragment. If a route is found, its corresponding component function replaces the content that is present in the main container. Otherwise, the generic notFound function is invoked. This method is called when the router starts and every time the hashchange event is fired. Figure 7-3 shows a diagram of the router's flow.

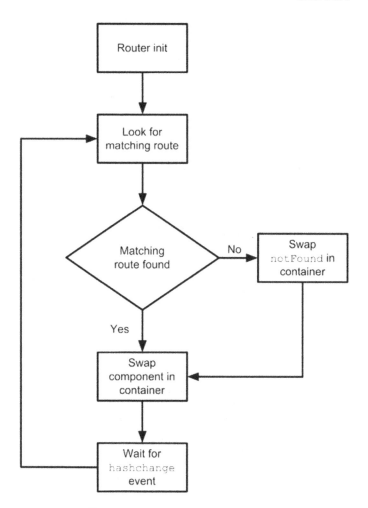

Figure 7-3. *Router flow*

Navigating Programmatically

In the previous example, the navigation is activated by clicking an anchor. Sometimes, you need to change the view *programmatically*. Think, for example, of redirecting the user to their personal page after a successful login. To do that, let's change the application a bit, as shown in Listing 7-6, swapping the links in the header with buttons.

155

Listing 7-6. Using Buttons to Navigate

```
<body>
    <header>
        <button data-navigate="/">
          Go To Index
        </button>
        <button data-navigate="/list">
          Go To List
        </button>
        <button data-navigate="/dummy">
        Dummy Page
      </button>
    </header>
    <main>
    </main>
</body>
```

Now you have to add an event handler for the buttons in the controller, as shown in Listing 7-7.

Listing 7-7. Adding Navigation to Buttons

```
const NAV_BTN_SELECTOR = 'button[data-navigate]'

document
  .body
  .addEventListener('click', e => {
    const { target } = e
    if (target.matches(NAV_BTN_SELECTOR)) {
      const { navigate } = target.dataset
      router.navigate(navigate)
    }
  })
```

To navigate to another view programmatically, I created a new public method for the router. This method gets the new fragment and replaces it in the location object. You can see the code of the navigate method in Listing 7-8.

Listing 7-8. Navigating Programmatically

```
router.navigate = fragment => {
  window.location.hash = fragment
}
```

It's quite important to wrap this line in a function to keep a standard interface when changing the internals of the router.

Route Parameters

The last feature that you will add to this router is reading route parameters. A route parameter is a part of the URL that is relative to some domain variable. For example, from the URL http://localhost:8080#/order/1, you can get the ID of an "order" domain model from it. In this case, 1 is a route parameter called id.

When creating a route with a parameter, to indicate that the URL will contain a parameter, this form is normally used: http://localhost:8080#/user/:id. I will stick to this *de facto* standard in this implementation.

The first thing that you need to do is slightly modify the component, as shown in Listing 7-9, in order to let it accept an argument. This argument will be filled with route parameters.

Listing 7-9. Components with Parameters

```
const detail = (params) => {
  const { id } = params
  container
```

```
    .textContent = '
      This is Detail Page with Id ${id}
    '
}

const anotherDetail = (params) => {
  const { id, anotherId } = params
  container
    .textContent = '
      This is another Detail Page with Id ${id}
      and AnotherId ${anotherId}
    '
}
```

Listing 7-10 shows how to bind these two new components with the relative URLs.

Listing 7-10. Defining Routes with Parameters

```
router
  .addRoute('#/', pages.home)
  .addRoute('#/list', pages.list)
  .addRoute('#/list/:id', pages.detail)
  .addRoute('#/list/:id/:anotherId', pages.anotherDetail)
  .setNotFound(pages.notFound)
  .start()
```

Now it's time to modify the router implementation in order to manage the route parameters. This implementation will be strongly based on regular expressions (RegEx). If you feel uncomfortable with regular expressions (like I do), I suggest using regex101,[2] a beneficial tool to grasp what a specific regular expression does.

---

[2] https://regex101.com/

The first thing to do is extract the parameter names from the URL that is used as the first argument of the addRoute method. For example, from #/list/:id/:anotherId, you have to extract an array with id and anotherId. You can see how to do that in Listing 7-11.

Listing 7-11. Extracting Parameter Names from Fragments

```
const ROUTE_PARAMETER_REGEXP = /:(\w+)/g
const URL_FRAGMENT_REGEXP = '([^\\/]+)'

router.addRoute = (fragment, component) => {
  const params = []

  const parsedFragment = fragment
    .replace(
      ROUTE_PARAMETER_REGEXP,
      (match, paramName) => {
        params.push(paramName)
        return URL_FRAGMENT_REGEXP
      })
    .replace(/\//g, '\\/')

  routes.push({
    testRegExp: new RegExp('^${parsedFragment}$'),
    component,
    params
  })

  return router
}
```

To extract parameter names from the fragment, use the /:(\w+)/g RegEx, which matches :id and :anotherId. You can use this schema to understand the purpose of this RegEx better.

:(\w+)

- : matches the exact character :

- ( ) indicates the start of a capturing group

- \w is a shortcut for [a-zA-Z0-9_] and matches any standard character

- + indicates that you accept at least one occurrence of a standard character

This RegEx is used with the replace function of the String object. For every match of the RegEx with the target String (in this case, the fragment), the callback is called. The second argument of this callback is the name of the parameter that you add to the params array. Then the match is replaced with another RegEx snippet: ([^\\/]+). At last, you wrap your new fragment between a ^ and a $.

So, passing the fragment #/list/:id/:anotherId as an argument to the addRoute method will result in a testRegExp with the value ^#\/list\/([^\\/]+)\/([^\\/]+)$ that you will use when checking if this route matches the current fragment in the location object. Here's a schema that explains in detail the meaning of this RegEx.

^#\/list\/([^\\/]+)\/([^\\/]+)$

- ^ indicates the beginning of the string

- #\/list\/ matches the exact string '#/list/'

- ( ) indicates the start of the first capturing group

  - [^\\/] matches any character apart from / and \

  - + indicates that you accept at least one occurrence of the previous match

- ( ) indicates the start of the second capturing group

  - [^\\/] matches any character apart from / and \

  - + indicates that you accept at least one occurrence of the previous match

- $ indicates the end of the string

In Listing 7-12, the generated regular expressions are used to select the right route for the current fragment and extract the actual parameters.

Listing 7-12. Extracting the URL Params from the Current Fragment

```
const extractUrlParams = (route, windowHash) => {
  if (route.params.length === 0) {
    return {}
  }

  const params = {}

  const matches = windowHash
    .match(route.testRegExp)

  matches.shift()

  matches.forEach((paramValue, index) => {
    const paramName = route.params[index]
    params[paramName] = paramValue
  })

  return params
}

const checkRoutes = () => {
  const { hash } = window.location
```

```
const currentRoute = routes.find(route => {
  const { testRegExp } = route
  return testRegExp.test(hash)
})

if (!currentRoute) {
  notFound()
  return
}

const urlParams = extractUrlParams(
  currentRoute,
  window.location.hash
)

currentRoute.component(urlParams)
}
```

As you can see, `testRegExp` checks if the current fragment matches one of the routes in the registry. It uses the same RegEx to extract the parameters that will be used as arguments for the component functions.

Notice the use of the `shift` in `extractUrlParams`. The `String.matches` method returns an array where the first element is the match itself, while the other elements are the result of the capturing groups. With `shift`, you remove the first element from that array.

This is a recap of what happens when managing a route with parameters.

- The fragment `#/list/:id/:anotherId` is passed to the `addRoute` method.

- This method extracts the parameter names (`id` and `anotherId`) and transforms the fragment in the RegEx `^#\/list\/([^\\/]+)\/([^\\/]+)$`.

- When the user navigates a matching fragment like #/list/1/2, the checkRoutes method selects the right route, thanks to the RegEx.

- The extractUrlParams method extracts the actual parameters from the current fragment in this object {id:'1', anotherId:'2'}.

- This object is passed to the component function that will update the DOM.

Figure 7-4 shows what the user gets when navigating to #/list/1/2.

Figure 7-4. Example project with route parameters

Listing 7-13 shows the complete code of the router based on fragment identifiers.

Listing 7-13. Router Based on Fragment Identifiers

```
const ROUTE_PARAMETER_REGEXP = /:(\w+)/g
const URL_FRAGMENT_REGEXP = '([^\\/]+)'

const extractUrlParams = (route, windowHash) => {
  const params = {}

  if (route.params.length === 0) {
    return params
  }

  const matches = windowHash
    .match(route.testRegExp)
```

```
  matches.shift()

  matches.forEach((paramValue, index) => {
    const paramName = route.params[index]
    params[paramName] = paramValue
  })

  return params
}
export default () => {
  const routes = []
  let notFound = () => {}

  const router = {}

  const checkRoutes = () => {
    const { hash } = window.location

    const currentRoute = routes.find(route => {
      const { testRegExp } = route
      return testRegExp.test(hash)
    })

    if (!currentRoute) {
      notFound()
      return
    }

    const urlParams = extractUrlParams(
      currentRoute,
      window.location.hash
    )

    currentRoute.component(urlParams)
  }
```

```
router.addRoute = (fragment, component) => {
  const params = []

  const parsedFragment = fragment
    .replace(
      ROUTE_PARAMETER_REGEXP,
      (match, paramName) => {
        params.push(paramName)
        return URL_FRAGMENT_REGEXP
      })
    .replace(/\//g, '\\/')

  console.log(`^${parsedFragment}$`)

  routes.push({
    testRegExp: new RegExp(`^${parsedFragment}$`),
    component,
    params
  })

  return router
}

router.setNotFound = cb => {
  notFound = cb
  return router
}

router.navigate = fragment => {
  window.location.hash = fragment
}

router.start = () => {
  window
    .addEventListener(
```

165

```
      'hashchange',
      checkRoutes
    )

  if (!window.location.hash) {
    window.location.hash = '#/'
  }

  checkRoutes()
  }

  return router
}
```

Note   This public API of this first implementation is the basis of the other implementations covered in this chapter.

The History API

History is an API that lets developers manipulate the browsing history of the user. For this second implementation of the router, you are going to use this API or, to be exact, one of its methods. Table 7-1 is a small cheat sheet of the History API.[3]

---

[3] For a complete reference, I suggest taking a look at the dedicated page on the Mozilla Development Network (https://developer.mozilla.org/en-US/docs/Web/API/History).

Table 7-1. *History API Cheat Sheet*

Signature	Description
back()	Go to the previous page in history.
forward()	Go to the next page in history.
go(index)	Go to a specific page in history.
pushState(state, title, URL)	Push the data in the history stack and navigate to the provided URL.
replaceState(state, title, URL)	Replace the most recent data in the history stack and navigate to the provided URL.

When using the History API for routing, you don't need to base your routes on fragment identifiers. You can instead utilize a real URL like http://localhost:8080/list/1/2. Listing 7-14 shows a version based on this API.

Listing 7-14. Router Built with the History API

```
const ROUTE_PARAMETER_REGEXP = /:(\w+)/g
const URL_FRAGMENT_REGEXP = '([^\\/]+)'
const TICKTIME = 250

const extractUrlParams = (route, pathname) => {
  const params = {}

  if (route.params.length === 0) {
    return params
  }

  const matches = pathname
    .match(route.testRegExp)

  matches.shift()
```

```
  matches.forEach((paramValue, index) => {
    const paramName = route.params[index]
    params[paramName] = paramValue
  })

  return params
}

export default () => {
  const routes = []
  let notFound = () => {}
  let lastPathname

  const router = {}

  const checkRoutes = () => {
    const { pathname } = window.location
    if (lastPathname === pathname) {
      return
    }

    lastPathname = pathname

    const currentRoute = routes.find(route => {
      const { testRegExp } = route
      return testRegExp.test(pathname)
    })

    if (!currentRoute) {
      notFound()
      return
    }

    const urlParams = extractUrlParams(currentRoute, pathname)

    currentRoute.callback(urlParams)
  }
```

```
router.addRoute = (path, callback) => {
  const params = []

  const parsedPath = path
    .replace(
      ROUTE_PARAMETER_REGEXP,
      (match, paramName) => {
        params.push(paramName)
        return URL_FRAGMENT_REGEXP
      })
    .replace(/\//g, '\\/')

  routes.push({
    testRegExp: new RegExp('^${parsedPath}$'),
    callback,
    params
  })

  return router
}

router.setNotFound = cb => {
  notFound = cb
  return router
}

router.navigate = path => {
  window
    .history
    .pushState(null, null, path)
}
```

```
router.start = () => {
  checkRoutes()
  window.setInterval(checkRoutes, TICKTIME)
}

return router
}
```

Let's look at the differences between this and the previous version based on fragment identifiers. The only method that you need from the History API is pushState to navigate to a new URL. The greatest difference between the previous implementation is the absence of a DOM event that you can employ to be notified when the URL changes. To achieve a similar result, you can use a setInterval to regularly check if the pathname is changed.

The public API is unchanged. The only thing that you need to change is the routes, removing the hash at the beginning, as in Listing 7-15.

Listing 7-15. Defining Routes without Fragments

```
router
  .addRoute('/', pages.home)
  .addRoute('/list', pages.list)
  .addRoute('/list/:id', pages.detail)
  .addRoute('/list/:id/:anotherId', pages.anotherDetail)
  .setNotFound(pages.notFound)
  .start()
```

Using Links

To switch completely to the History API, you need to update the links in the template. Listing 7-16 is an updated version of the initial template of the sample application. In this case, the links point to real URLs and not to fragment identifiers on the same page.

Listing 7-16. History API Link Navigation

```
<header>
  <a href="/">Go To Index</a>
  <a href="/list">Go To List</a>
  <a href="/list/1">Go To Detail With Id 1</a>
  <a href="/list/2">Go To Detail With Id 2</a>
  <a href="/list/1/2">Go To Another Detail</a>
  <a href="/dummy">Dummy Page</a>
</header>
```

Just changing the href attribute is not enough; these links will not work as expected. For example, clicking the Go To List link will result in navigating to the http://localhost:8080/list/index.html URL, resulting in a 404 HTTP error.

In order to make these links work, you need to change their *default behavior*. The first thing to do is mark all the links that are used for internal navigation, as shown in Listing 7-17.

Listing 7-17. History API Link Navigation Marked Links

```
<header>
  <a data-navigation href="/">Go To Index</a>
  <a data-navigation href="/list">Go To List</a>
  <a data-navigation href="/list/1">Go To Detail With Id 1</a>
  <a data-navigation href="/list/2">Go To Detail With Id 2</a>
  <a data-navigation href="/list/1/2">Go To Another Detail</a>
  <a data-navigation href="/dummy">Dummy Page</a>
</header>
```

In Listing 7-18, you can easily recognize these links, disabling standard navigation and using the router's navigate method.

Listing 7-18. Changing the Behavior of the Internal
Navigation Links

```
const NAV_A_SELECTOR = 'a[data-navigation]'

router.start = () => {
  checkRoutes()
  window.setInterval(checkRoutes, TICKTIME)

  document
    .body
    .addEventListener('click', e => {
      const { target } = e
      if (target.matches(NAV_A_SELECTOR)) {
        e.preventDefault()
        router.navigate(target.href)
      }
    })

  return router
}
```

The router intercept clicks every internal navigation anchor, using the event delegation technique discussed in Chapter 3. It's possible to disable the standard handler of any DOM element with the preventDefault method of the Event object.

Navigo

The last implementation that you will learn about in this chapter is based on Navigo,[4] a very simple and small open-source library. As you learned in the previous chapter, it's very important to wrap libraries

---

[4]https://github.com/krasimir/navigo

with your own public interface. The implementation in Listing 7-19 keeps the same API of the previous two; it just changes the internals of the router.

Listing 7-19. Router Implementation with Navigo

```
export default () => {
  const navigoRouter = new window.Navigo()
  const router = {}

  router.addRoute = (path, callback) => {
    navigoRouter.on(path, callback)
    return router
  }

  router.setNotFound = cb => {
    navigoRouter.notFound(cb)
    return router
  }

  router.navigate = path => {
    navigoRouter.navigate(path)
  }

  router.start = () => {
    navigoRouter.resolve()
    return router
  }

  return router
}
```

Managing internal navigation links is very similar to the previous implementation. You just need to change data-navigation in data-navigo, as you can see in Listing 7-20.

Listing 7-20. Internal Navigation Links with Navigo

```
<header>
  <a data-navigo href="/">Go To Index</a>
  <a data-navigo href="/list">Go To List</a>
  <a data-navigo href="/list/1">Go To Detail With Id 1</a>
  <a data-navigo href="/list/2">Go To Detail With Id 2</a>
  <a data-navigo href="/list/1/2">Go To Another Detail</a>
  <a data-navigo href="/dummy">Dummy Page</a>
</header>
```

Choosing the Right Router

There's no meaningful difference between the three implementations. My suggestion is to start with a frameworkless implementation, and only if you need something *very complex,* switch to a third-party library.

Routing is the nervous system of any SPA; it decides how to match URLs with what users see on-screen. Keep this in mind when you're working with a framework. If you use React Router for a project, it means that, probably, you will not be able to remove React from your project, because it's very hard to change the routing system of an SPA. Nevertheless, if your routing system is independent, you can start changing the framework one view at a time.

Tip   When using a framework, try to keep a separate layer for routing.

Summary

In this chapter, you learned the meaning of a single page application and how to create a client-side routing system. You built two different frameworkless versions of a router, the first one based on fragment identifiers and the other one based on the History API. You also created a router based on Navigo, a very small JavaScript library.

The next chapter explains how to manage the state of your applications with different state management techniques.

CHAPTER 8

State Management

In the previous chapters, you learned how to display data, manage user inputs, and make HTTP requests and routes. You can consider these skills as basic *building blocks*. But before you can start writing frameworkless code, you need to know how to manage the data (or the *state*) that *links* all these elements together. In front-end applications or, more generally, all kinds of client applications (web, desktop, and mobile), the problem of effectively managing data is called *state management.*

State management doesn't solve a new problem, and indeed Model View Controller (the most famous state management pattern) was introduced in the 1970s. However, when React became a mainstream library, the term started appearing in blogs, conferences, and so on. Right now, there are a bunch of dedicated libraries for front-end state management. Some are tied to existing frameworks like pinia[1] (for Vue. js) and NgRx[2] (for Angular), while other libraries are agnostic, like Valtio[3] and Redux.

Choosing the right architecture for your state management code is crucial to keeping the application healthy and maintainable. In this chapter, you will build three state management strategies, compare them, and analyze their pros and cons.

---

[1] https://pinia.vuejs.org/
[2] https://ngrx.io/
[3] https://github.com/pmndrs/valtio

© Francesco Strazzullo 2023
F. Strazzullo, *Frameworkless Front-End Development,*
https://doi.org/10.1007/978-1-4842-9351-5_8

Reviewing the TodoMVC Application

The examples in this chapter use the TodoMVC that you developed in Chapter 3 with a functional rendering engine. In Listing 8-1, you can see the controller's code with all the events that manipulate the todos and the filter.[4]

Listing 8-1. The TodoMVC Controller

```
import todosView from './view/todos.js'
import counterView from './view/counter.js'
import filtersView from './view/filters.js'
import appView from './view/app.js'
import applyDiff from './applyDiff.js'

import registry from './registry.js'

registry.add('app', appView)
registry.add('todos', todosView)
registry.add('counter', counterView)
registry.add('filters', filtersView)

const state = {
  todos: [],
  currentFilter: 'All'
}

const events = {
  addItem: text => {
    state.todos.push({
      text,
```

---

[4] The complete code of this application is available at https://github.com/ Apress/Frameworkless-Front-End-Development-2nd-ed./tree/main/ Chapter08/00.

```
      completed: false
    })
    render()
  },
  updateItem: (index, text) => {
    state.todos[index].text = text
    render()
  },
  deleteItem: (index) => {
    state.todos.splice(index, 1)
    render()
  },
  toggleItemCompleted: (index) => {
    const {
      completed
    } = state.todos[index]
    state.todos[index].completed = !completed
    render()
  },
  completeAll: () => {
    state.todos.forEach(t => {
      t.completed = true
    })
    render()
  },
  clearCompleted: () => {
    state.todos = state.todos.filter(
      t => !t.completed
    )
    render()
  },
```

```
  changeFilter: filter => {
    state.currentFilter = filter
    render()
  }
}

const render = () => {
  window.requestAnimationFrame(() => {
    const main = document.querySelector('#root')

    const newMain = registry.renderRoot(
      main,
      state,
      events)

    applyDiff(document.body, main, newMain)
  })
}

render()
```

The state management code is defined in the events object that you pass to the View function to attach its methods to DOM handlers.

Model View Controller

Keeping your state in the controllers is not a good way to manage it. The first step to enhance this design is to move all that code into a separate file. Moving it to an external file has various advantages; the most important one is testability. Having a separate model file lets developers work just with the data of the model and not its presentation. In Listing 8-2, you can see an updated version of the controller with an external model that manages the state of the application.

Listing 8-2. The Controller with a Separate Model

```
import modelFactory from './model/model.js'

const model = modelFactory()

const events = {
  addItem: text => {
    model.addItem(text)
    render(model.getState())
  },
  updateItem: (index, text) => {
    model.updateItem(index, text)
    render(model.getState())
  },
  deleteItem: (index) => {
    model.deleteItem(index)
    render(model.getState())
  },
  toggleItemCompleted: (index) => {
    model.toggleItemCompleted(index)
    render(model.getState())
  },
  completeAll: () => {
    model.completeAll()
    render(model.getState())
  },
  clearCompleted: () => {
    model.clearCompleted()
    render(model.getState())
  },
  changeFilter: filter => {
    model.changeFilter(filter)
```

```
    render(model.getState())
  }
}

const render = (state) => {
  window.requestAnimationFrame(() => {
    const main = document.querySelector('#root')

    const newMain = registry.renderRoot(
      main,
      state,
      events)

    applyDiff(document.body, main, newMain)
  })
}
```

render(**model.getState()**)

Notice that the actual data used to render is returned from the getState method of the model object. In Listing 8-3, you can see its code. For simplicity, this listing just includes the addItem and the updateItem methods[5] (this is also true in other listings regarding the model in this chapter).

Listing 8-3. Simple Model Object for the TodoMVC Application

```
const INITIAL_STATE = {
  todos: [],
  currentFilter: 'All'
}
```

---

[5] To check the complete code you can visit the GitHub repository at https:// github.com/Apress/Frameworkless-Front-End-Development-2nd-ed./blob/ main/Chapter08/00/model/model.js.

```
export default (initalState = INITIAL_STATE) => {
  const state = structuredClone(initalState)

  const getState = () => {
    return Object.freeze(structuredClone(state))
  }

  const addItem = text => {
    if (!text) {
      return
    }

    state.todos.push({
      text,
      completed: false
    })
  }

  const updateItem = (index, text) => {
    if (!text) {
      return
    }

    if (index < 0) {
      return
    }

    if (!state.todos[index]) {
      return
    }

    state.todos[index].text = text
  }
```

```
//Other methods...

return {
  addItem,
  updateItem,
  deleteItem,
  toggleItemCompleted,
  completeAll,
  clearCompleted,
  changeFilter,
  getState
  }
}
```

Values from a model object should be *immutable*. This code generates a clone every time that getState is invoked and freezes it with Object. freeze.[6] To clone the object, use structuredClone,[7] which creates a deep clone of a given object. Using an immutable state to transfer data forces the consumers of this API to use public methods to manipulate the state itself. In this way, the business logic is completely contained in the model object and not scattered in various parts of the application. This approach helps the state management code have high testability during the lifespan of the codebase. In Listing 8-4, you can see part of the test suite of the model object.

---

[6]https://developer.mozilla.org/it/docs/Web/JavaScript/Reference/
Global_Objects/Object/freeze
[7]https://developer.mozilla.org/en-US/docs/Web/API/structuredClone

Listing 8-4. Test Suite for the TodoMVC State Object

```
import stateFactory from './state.js'

describe('external state', () => {
  test('data should be immutable', () => {
    const state = stateFactory()

    expect(() => {
      state.get().currentFilter = 'WRONG'
    }).toThrow()
  })

  test('should add an item', () => {
    const state = stateFactory()

    state.addItem('dummy')

    const { todos } = state.get()

    expect(todos.length).toBe(1)
    expect(todos[0]).toEqual({
      text: 'dummy',
      completed: false
    })
  })

  test('should not add an item when a falsy text is
  provided', () => {
    const state = stateFactory()

    state.addItem('')
    state.addItem(undefined)
    state.addItem(0)
    state.addItem()
    state.addItem(false)
```

```
    const { todos } = state.get()

    expect(todos.length).toBe(0)
  })

  test('should update an item', () => {
    const state = stateFactory({
      todos: [{
        text: 'dummy',
        completed: false
      }]
    })

    state.updateItem(0, 'new-dummy')

    const { todos } = state.get()

    expect(todos[0].text).toBe('new-dummy')
  })

  test('should not update an item when an invalid index is
  provided', () => {
    const state = stateFactory({
      todos: [{
        text: 'dummy',
        completed: false
      }]
    })

    state.updateItem(1, 'new-dummy')

    const { todos } = state.get()

    expect(todos[0].text).toBe('dummy')
  })
})
```

This first version of a state management library for the TodoMVC application is a classic Model View Controller (MVC) implementation. Historically, MVC was probably one of the first patterns dedicated to managing the state of a client application. You can see a schema of this pattern in Figure 8-1.

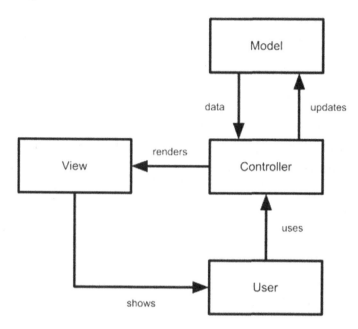

Figure 8-1. *MVC pattern schema*

This model object will be the base for all the other implementations. Before continuing, let's review the workflow of the application and the relationship between its parts.

- The controller gets the initial state from the model.

- The controller invokes the view to render the initial state.

- The system is ready to receive user inputs.

187

- The user does something (for example, they add an item).

- The controller maps the user action with the correct model method (`model.addItem`).

- The model updates the state.

- The controller gets the new state from the model.

- The controller invokes the view to render the new state.

- The system is ready to receive user inputs.

This workflow is quite generic for any front-end application, and it is summarized in Figure 8-2. The loop between the render and the user action is called the "render cycle."

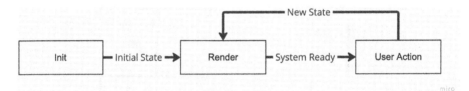

Figure 8-2. *The render cycle*

Observable Model

This first version of state management code based on MVC works quite well for this use case. Nevertheless, the integration between the model and the controller is quite clumsy: you need to *manually* invoke the render method every time the user takes some kind of action. This is not an optimal solution for two main reasons. The first one is that manually invoking the render after every state change is a very error-prone approach. The second one is that the render method is also invoked when the action does not modify the state. For example, when adding an empty item to the list. Both these issues are resolved in the next version of the model, which is based on the observer[8] pattern.

In Listing 8-5, you can see the new version of the model. The differences from the previous version are highlighted for better readability.[9]

Listing 8-5. The Observable TodoMVC Model

```
const INITIAL_STATE = {
  todos: [],
  currentFilter: 'All'
}

export default (initalState = INITIAL_STATE) => {
  const state = structuredClone(initalState)
  let listeners = []

  const addChangeListener = listener => {
    listeners.push(listener)

    listener(freeze(state))

    return () => {
      listeners = listeners.filter(
        l => l !== listener
      )
    }
  }
```

[8] https://en.wikipedia.org/wiki/Observer_pattern

[9] The complete code is available at https://github.com/Apress/frameworkless-front-end-development/blob/master/Chapter08/01/model/model.js.

```
const invokeListeners = () => {
  const data = freeze(state)
  listeners.forEach(l => l(data))
}

const addItem = text => {
  if (!text) {
    return
  }

  state.todos.push({
    text,
    completed: false
  })

  invokeListeners()
}

const updateItem = (index, text) => {
  if (!text) {
    return
  }

  if (index < 0) {
    return
  }

  if (!state.todos[index]) {
    return
  }

  state.todos[index].text = text

  invokeListeners()
}
```

```
  //Other methods...

  return {
    addItem,
    updateItem,
    deleteItem,
    toggleItemCompleted,
    completeAll,
    clearCompleted,
    changeFilter,
    addChangeListener
  }
}
```

In order to easily understand the public API of this observable model you can use Listing 8-6, which shows a simple test suite for the new model.

Listing 8-6. Unit Tests for the Observable Model

```
import modelFactory from './model.js'
let model

describe('observable model', () => {
  beforeEach(() => {
    model = modelFactory()
  })

  test('listeners should be invoked immediately', () => {
    let counter = 0
    model.addChangeListener(data => {
      counter++
    })
    expect(counter).toBe(1)
  })
```

```
test('listeners should be invoked when changing
data', () => {
  let counter = 0
  model.addChangeListener(data => {
    counter++
  })
  model.addItem('dummy')
  expect(counter).toBe(2)
})

test('listeners should be removed when
unsubscribing', () => {
  let counter = 0
  const unsubscribe = model
  .addChangeListener(data => {
      counter++
    })
  unsubscribe()
  model.addItem('dummy')
  expect(counter).toBe(1)
})

test('state should be immutable', () => {
  model.addChangeListener(data => {
    expect(() => {
      data.currentFilter = 'WRONG'
    }).toThrow()
  })
})
})
```

Reading the tests, it's clear that the only way to get the state from the Model object is to add a listener callback. This callback will be invoked at the moment of subscription and every time the internal state changes. This approach will simplify the controller, as you can see in Listing 8-7.

Listing 8-7. Using an Observable Model in the Controller

```
import modelFactory from './model/model.js'

const model = modelFactory()

const {
  addChangeListener,
  ...events
} = model

const render = (state) => {
  window.requestAnimationFrame(() => {
    const main = document.querySelector('#root')

    const newMain = registry.renderRoot(
      main,
      state,
      events)

    applyDiff(document.body, main, newMain)
  })
}
```

addChangeListener(render)

The controller code is much simpler now. To bind the render method to the model, it's enough to use that method as a listener for the model. Notice that the methods are extracted from the model (apart from addEventListener) to use them as events that you pass to the view.

Having an observable model is useful for adding new features to the controller without modifying the public interface of the model. Listing 8-8 shows a new version of the controller that creates two new change listeners. The first one is a simple logger on the console. The second one saves the state to window.localStorage. In this way, the controller can load the initial data from the storage when the application starts.

Listing 8-8. More Listeners Used with the Observable Model

```
import stateFactory from './model/state.js'

const loadState = () => {
  const serializedState = window
    .localStorage
    .getItem('state')

  if (!serializedState) {
    return
  }

  return JSON.parse(serializedState)
}

const state = stateFactory(loadState())

const {
  addChangeListener,
  ...events
} = state

const render = (state) => {
  // Render Code
}

addChangeListener(render)
```

```
addChangeListener(state => {
  Promise.resolve().then(() => {
    window
      .localStorage
      .setItem('state', JSON.stringify(state))
  })
})

addChangeListener(state => {
  console.log(
    'Current State (${(new Date()).getTime()})',
    state
  )
})
```

To implement the same features without the observable model would have been really difficult and not maintainable. Remember this pattern when your controller becomes *too coupled* with the model.

Before continuing, it's important to state that in this section, I always state "the model" as it was a single object. This is true for a simple application like TodoMVC. In a real scenario, "the model" is a collection of Model objects that manage all the different domains in your application.

Reactive Programming

Reactive programming has been a buzzword in the front-end community for quite a while. It became trendy when the Angular team announced that their framework would have to be heavily based on RxJS (an acronym for "React Extensions for JavaScript"), a library built to create applications based on Reactive programming.[10]

In a nutshell, implementing the Reactive paradigm means working in an application where everything is an observable that can *emit* events: model changes, HTTP requests, user actions, navigation, and so on.

Tip   If you're using a lot of observables in your code, you're working with a Reactive paradigm.

Reactive programming is a fascinating and deep topic, and this chapter just scratches the surface, creating a Reactive state management library in a couple of different ways. If you'd like to study this topic in depth, I suggest reading *Front-End Reactive Architectures* by Luca Mezzalira.[11]

A Reactive Model

The model created in Listing 8-5 is already an example of Reactive state management because it's an observable. But, in a non-trivial application, there should be a lot of different model objects, and so you need an easy way to create observables. In this way, you can focus on the domain logic, leaving the architectural part in a separate library. In Listing 8-9, you can see a new version of the model object based on an observable factory, while Listing 8-10 shows the observable factory itself.

---

[10] In my opinion, the best source to easily understand the meaning of Reactive programming is this GitHub Gist (`https://gist.github.com/staltz/868e7e9bc2a7b8c1f754`) titled "The Introduction to Reactive Programming You've Been Missing," by André Staltz, one of the maintainers of RxJS.

[11] `www.apress.com/gp/book/9781484231791`

Listing 8-9. An Observable TodoMVC Model Built with a Factory

```
import observableFactory from './observable.js'

const INITIAL_STATE = {
  todos: [],
  currentFilter: 'All'
}

export default (initalState = INITIAL_STATE) => {
  const state = structuredClone(initalState)

  const addItem = text => {
    if (!text) {
      return
    }

    state.todos.push({
      text,
      completed: false
    })
  }

  const updateItem = (index, text) => {
    if (!text) {
      return
    }

    if (index < 0) {
      return
    }

    if (!state.todos[index]) {
      return
    }
```

```
    state.todos[index].text = text
  }

  ...

  const model = {
    addItem,
    updateItem,
    deleteItem,
    toggleItemCompleted,
    completeAll,
    clearCompleted,
    changeFilter
  }

  return observableFactory(model, () => state)
}
```

Listing 8-10. An Observable Factory

```
export default (model, stateGetter) => {
  let listeners = []

  const addChangeListener = cb => {
    listeners.push(cb)
    cb(freeze(stateGetter()))
    return () => {
      listeners = listeners
        .filter(element => element !== cb)
    }
  }
```

```javascript
const invokeListeners = () => {
  const data = freeze(stateGetter())
  listeners.forEach(l => l(data))
}

const wrapAction = originalAction => {
  return (...args) => {
    const value = originalAction(...args)
    invokeListeners()
    return value
  }
}

const baseProxy = {
  addChangeListener
}

return Object
  .keys(model)
  .filter(key => {
    return typeof model[key] === 'function'
  })
  .reduce((proxy, key) => {
    const action = model[key]
    return {
      ...proxy,
      [key]: wrapAction(action)
    }
  }, baseProxy)
}
```

The code of the observable factory may seem a little obscure, but its functioning is quite simple. It creates a *proxy* of the model object that, for every method of the original model, creates a new method with the same name that wraps the original one and invokes all the listeners. To pass the state to the proxy, a simple getter function is used to get the current state after every modification made by the model.

From an external point of view, the observable model in Listing 8-5 and the one in Listing 8-9 have the same public interface. A good way to design a reactive state management architecture is to create a simple observable model, and only when you need more than one Model object do you create the observable factory abstraction. Figure 8-3 shows the relationship between the controller, the model, and the proxy.

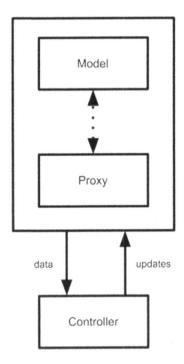

Figure 8-3. *Observable model with a proxy*

Native Proxies

JavaScript has a native way to create proxies, via the Proxy object.[12] Using this new AP is quite easy. You wrap the default behavior of any object with some custom code. Listing 8-11 creates a simple proxy that logs a message every time you get or set a property of the base object. Figure 8-4 shows the result in the browser's console.

Listing 8-11. Basic Proxy Object Usage

```
const base = {
  foo: 'bar'
}

const handler = {
  get: (target, name) => {
    console.log('Getting ${name}')
    return target[name]
  },
  set: (target, name, value) => {
    console.log('Setting ${name} to ${value}')
    target[name] = value
    return true
  }
}

const proxy = new Proxy(base, handler)

proxy.foo = 'baz'
console.log('Logging ${proxy.foo}')
```

---

[12] https://developer.mozilla.org/en-US/docs/Web/JavaScript/Reference/
Global_Objects/Proxy

		Elements	Console	Sources	Network	Performance	Memory	Application	Security	Audits

```
▶  ⊘  | top              ▼   ⊙  | Filter                        Default levels ▼
    Setting foo to baz
    Getting foo
    Logging baz
  >
```

Figure 8-4. *Basic proxy result*

In order to create a proxy that wraps a base object, you need to provide a handler that consists of a set of traps. A *trap* is a method that wraps a basic operation on the base object. This simple case overwrote all the properties' setters and getters. Notice that the set handler should return a Boolean value that represents the success of the operation. Listings 8-12 uses the Proxy object to create an observable factory.

Listing 8-12. Observable Factory with Proxy Object.freeze

```
export default (initialState) => {
  let listeners = []

  const proxy = new Proxy(structuredClone(initialState), {
    set: (target, name, value) => {
      target[name] = value
      listeners.forEach(l => l(freeze(proxy)))
      return true
    }
  })

  proxy.addChangeListener = cb => {
    listeners.push(cb)
    cb(freeze(proxy))
    return () => {
      listeners = listeners.filter(l => l !== cb)
```

```
    }
  }

  return proxy
}
```

Even if the signature is similar, the usage is slightly different, as in Listing 8-13. It shows the new version of the model created with this new observable factory.

Listing 8-13. An Observable TodoMVC Model Built with a Proxy Factory

```
export default (initialState = INITIAL_STATE) => {
  const state = observableFactory(initialState)

  const addItem = text => {
    if (!text) {
      return
    }

    state.todos = [...state.todos, {
      text,
      completed: false
    }]
  }

  const updateItem = (index, text) => {
    if (!text) {
      return
    }

    if (index < 0) {
      return
    }
```

```
  if (!state.todos[index]) {
    return
  }

  state.todos = state.todos.map((todo, i) => {
    if (i === index) {
      todo.text = text
    }
    return todo
  })
}

...

return {
  addChangeListener: state.addChangeListener,
  addItem,
  updateItem,
  deleteItem,
  toggleItemCompleted,
  completeAll,
  clearCompleted,
  changeFilter
}
}
```

There's a significant difference between the two versions. In this second one, based on Proxy, the todos array is *overwritten* every time. In the first one, the todos array is modified in place, invoking the Array's push method or substituting an element. When using a Proxy object, it's mandatory to overwrite the properties in order to invoke the set trap.

Caution   When working with a `Proxy` object, always replace properties instead of modifying them in place.

Event Bus

This section covers how to manage the state of an application using the Event Bus pattern. Event Bus is one possible way to implement an Event-driven architecture (EDA). When working with EDAs, every state change is represented by an event that is dispatched in the system.[13] An event is defined by a name that identifies what happened and a payload containing meaningful information to process the event. In Listing 8-14, you can see an example event that should be dispatched when creating a new item in the TodoMVC domain.

Listing 8-14. Add Item Event

```
const event = {
  type: 'ITEM_ADDED',
  payload: 'Buy Milk'
}
```

The main idea behind the Event Bus pattern is that every event is processed by a single object that connects all the "nodes" that compose the application. The event is then processed, and the result is sent to all the connected nodes. When using an Event Bus for state management, the result of any event processing is an updated version of the application's state. Figure 8-5 shows a diagram of the Event Bus pattern.

---

[13] To learn more about the various kinds of EDA and their differences, I suggest reading *Building Evolutionary Architectures: Support Constant Change* at `www.amazon.com/Building-Evolutionary-Architectures-Support-Constant/dp/1491986360` by Neal Ford, Rebecca Parsons and Patrick Kua.

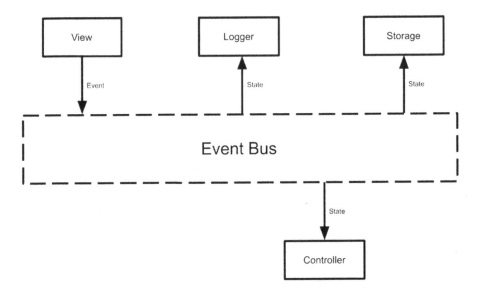

Figure 8-5. *The Event Bus pattern*

To better understand how an Event Bus works, you can analyze the flow of an ITEM_ADDED event:

- The view renders the initial state.

- The user fills in the form and presses Enter.

- The DOM event is captured by the view.

- The view creates the ITEM_ADDED event and dispatches it to the bus.

- The bus processes the event, generating a new state.

- The new state is sent to the controller.

- The controller invokes the view to render the new state.

- The system is ready to receive user inputs.

I just stated that the bus "processes the event, generating a new state." This is not correct because the Event Bus is an architectural element and *should not contain any kind of domain-related code*. You need to add the model to the mix in order to implement the Event Bus pattern. In this scenario, the model is a function that accepts the old state and an event and returns a new version of the state, as shown in Figure 8-6.

It's important to note that, in this pattern, the state that travels from the model to the subscribers is a single object. This object contains all the data useful for the application. This does not mean that the model should be one single, big JavaScript function. You will see later how it's possible to split this model into sub-models that together build the state object.

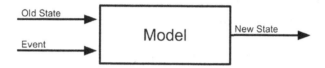

Figure 8-6. *Model structure in an Event Bus application*

Figure 8-7 shows an updated diagram of the Event Bus pattern, with the addition of the model.

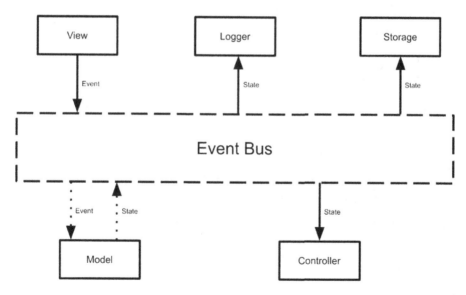

Figure 8-7. *Event Bus pattern with model*

To complete this section, you will analyze two Event Bus implementations. The first one is a frameworkless one, while the second one is based on Redux. Redux is a state management library born in the React ecosystem but usable in any kind of environment.

A Frameworkless Implementation

The first element you will analyze is the Event Bus itself. As with the previous examples, not all of the code is shown here.[14] You can see the code of the Event Bus in Listing 8-15.

Listing 8-15. Frameworkless Event Bus

```
export default (model) => {
  let listeners = []
  let state = model()

  const subscribe = listener => {
    listeners.push(listener)

    return () => {
      listeners = listeners
        .filter(l => l !== listener)
    }
  }

  const invokeSubscribers = () => {
    const data = freeze(state)
    listeners.forEach(l => l(data))
  }
```

---

[14] The complete code of this implementation is available at https://github.com/ Apress/frameworkless-front-end-development/tree/master/Chapter07/03.

```
const dispatch = event => {
  const newState = model(state, event)

  if (!newState) {
    throw new Error('model should always return a value')
  }

  if (newState === state) {
    return
  }

  state = newState

  invokeSubscribers()
}
return {
  subscribe,
  dispatch,
  getState: () => freeze(state)
}
}
```

In this scenario, the model is a function that gets the previous state and the event as inputs and returns a new state. There is another important characteristic of the model; it's a pure function. A pure function is a function where the return value is only determined by its input values, just like any standard mathematical function like Math.cos(x).

To design the model as a pure function provides a big boost to testability. Because the new state cannot depend on the internal status of the model itself. You can also use this aspect to optimize performance, because every time the state is updated, it has to be a new object. So if the old state and new state are equal, it means that you can skip the subscribers. In this implementation, invoking the model without parameters will result in obtaining the *application's initial state.*

To better understand the inner workings of the Event Bus, Listing 8-16 shows the related test suite.

Listing 8-16. Test Suite for the Event Bus

```
import eventBusFactory from './eventBus'
let eventBus

const counterModel = (state, event) => {
  if (!event) {
    return {
      counter: 0
    }
  }

  if (event.type !== 'COUNTER') {
    return state
  }

  return {
    counter: state.counter++
  }
}

describe('eventBus', () => {
  beforeEach(() => {
    eventBus = eventBusFactory(counterModel)
  })

  test('subscribers should be invoked when the model catch the
  event', () => {
    let counter = 0

    eventBus.subscribe(() => counter++)

    eventBus.dispatch({ type: 'COUNTER' })
```

```
    expect(counter).toBe(1)
  })

  test('subscribers should not be invoked when the model does
  not catch the event', () => {
    let counter = 0

    eventBus.subscribe(() => counter++)

    eventBus.dispatch({ type: 'NOT_COUNTER' })

    expect(counter).toBe(0)
  })

  test('subscribers should receive an immutable state', () => {
    eventBus.dispatch({ type: 'COUNTER' })
    eventBus.subscribe((state) => {
      expect(() => {
        state.counter = 0
      }).toThrow()
    })
  })

  test('should throw error if the model does not return a
  state', () => {
    const eventBus = eventBusFactory(() => {
      return undefined
    })

    expect(() => {
      eventBus.dispatch({ type: 'EVENT' })
    }).toThrow()
  })
})
```

The counterModel object gives you a glimpse of how a model should work in an Event Bus architecture. When an event of the COUNTER type is dispatched, a new state is created with an incremented counter property. For all the other events, nothing is changed, and the old state is returned. Listing 8-17 shows part of the model of the TodoMVC application.

Listing 8-17. TodoMVC Model for Event Bus Architecture

```
const INITIAL_STATE = {
  todos: [],
  currentFilter: 'All'
}
const addItem = (state, event) => {
  const text = event.payload
  if (!text) {
    return state
  }

  return {
    ...state,
    todos: [...state.todos, {
      text,
      completed: false
    }]
  }
}
const updateItem = (state, event) => {
  const { text, index } = event.payload
  if (!text) {
    return state
  }
```

```
  if (index < 0) {
    return state
  }

  if (!state.todos[index]) {
    return state
  }

  return {
    ...state,
    todos: state.todos.map((todo, i) => {
      if (i === index) {
        todo.text = text
      }
      return todo
    })
  }
}

const methods = {
  ITEM_ADDED: addItem,
  ITEM_UPDATED: updateItem
}

export default (initalState = INITIAL_STATE) => {
  return (prevState, event) => {
    if (!prevState) {
      return structuredClone(initalState)
    }

    const currentMethod = methods[event.type]

    if (!currentMethod) {
      return prevState
    }
```

```
   return currentMethod(prevState, event)
  }
}
```

In order to avoid a very long switch statement to choose the right method based on the Event type, I used a simple object that maps the Event type with a method. If no method is found, it means that the model does not manage that event, and so the previous state is returned.

In the previous section, I stated that in a real application, the Model function should be separated into smaller sub-modules.[15] In that version of the model, there are two sub-models. The first one manages the todos, and the other one manages the filter. The main Model function merges the results of the sub-models into a single state object.

Tip   When working with an Event Bus, split the model into sub-models in order to achieve good code readability.

Listing 8-18 shows the controller of the TodoMVC application based on the Event Bus.

Listing 8-18. Controller of an Event Bus-Based TodoMVC Application

```
import eventBusFactory from './model/eventBus.js'
import modelFactory from './model/model.js'

const model = modelFactory()
const eventBus = eventBusFactory(model)
```

---

[15] You can see another version of the Model in Listing 8-17 on GitHub at https://github.com/Apress/frameworkless-front-end-development/blob/master/Chapter07/03.1/model/model.js.

```
const render = (state) => {
  window.requestAnimationFrame(() => {
    const main = document.querySelector('#root')

    const newMain = registry.renderRoot(
      main,
      state,
      eventBus.dispatch)

    applyDiff(document.body, main, newMain)
  })
}

eventBus.subscribe(render)

render(eventBus.getState())
```

As you can see, the major difference with previous versions is that it doesn't provide the events to the render function, but just the `dispatch` method of the Event Bus. In this way, the view is capable of dispatching events in the system, as you can see in Listing 8-19, which shows part of the code of the view.

Listing 8-19. View Function Using the Event Bus

```
import eventCreators from '../model/eventCreators.js'

let template

const getTemplate = () => {
  if (!template) {
    template = document.getElementById('todo-app')
  }
```

```
  return template
    .content
    .firstElementChild
    .cloneNode(true)
}

const addEvents = (targetElement, dispatch) => {
  targetElement
    .querySelector('.new-todo')
    .addEventListener('keypress', e => {
      if (e.key === 'Enter') {
        const event = eventCreators
          .addItem(e.target.value)
        dispatch(event)
        e.target.value = ''
      }
    })
}

export default (targetElement, state, dispatch) => {
  const newApp = targetElement.cloneNode(true)

  newApp.innerHTML = ''
  newApp.appendChild(getTemplate())

  addEvents(newApp, dispatch)

  return newApp
}
```

Notice the use of eventCreators.addItem to create the Event object to dispatch. The eventCreators object is a simple collection of factories used to easily build consistent events. You can see its code in Listing 8-20.

Listing 8-20. Event Creators

```
const EVENT_TYPES = Object.freeze({
  ITEM_ADDED: 'ITEM_ADDED',
  ITEM_UPDATED: 'ITEM_UPDATED'
})

export default {
  addItem: text => ({
    type: EVENT_TYPES.ITEM_ADDED,
    payload: text
  }),
  updateItem: (index, text) => ({
    type: EVENT_TYPES.ITEM_UPDATED,
    payload: {
      text,
      index
    }
  })
}
```

These functions are useful for ensuring that every event is in the canonical form shown in Listing 8-14.

Redux

Redux is a state management library that was first announced at the React-Europe conference in 2015 with a talk[16] by Dan Abramov. After that, it rapidly became a mainstream approach when working with React applications. Redux is one (and surely the most successful) of the so-called Flux-like libraries, a group of tools that implemented Facebook's

---

[16] www.youtube.com/watch?v=xsSnOQynTHs

architecture, Flux.[17] Working with Redux is very similar to working with a frameworkless Event Bus. Nevertheless, being born after the Flux pattern, the words used to define the components of the architecture are different, as you can see in Table 8-1.

Table 8-1. *Comparing the Event Bus and Redux Elements*

Event Bus	Redux
Event Bus	Store
Event	Action
Model	Reducer

To better understand the principles behind Redux, I strongly suggest reading the "Three Principles" chapter of the Redux documentation (`https://redux.js.org/introduction/three-principles`).

Apart from the naming, the elements are quite similar. In fact, in Listing 8-21, you can see the code of the controller of a TodoMVC application built with Redux.

Listing 8-21. Controller of a Redux-Based TodoMVC Application

```
import reducer from './model/reducer.js'

const INITIAL_STATE = {
  todos: [],
  currentFilter: 'All'
}

const {
  createStore
} = Redux
```

---

[17] To learn more about Flux, you can consult the official website at `https://facebook.github.io/flux/`.

```
const store = createStore(
  reducer,
  INITIAL_STATE
)

const render = () => {
  window.requestAnimationFrame(() => {
    const main = document.querySelector('#root')

    const newMain = registry.renderRoot(
      main,
      store.getState(),
      store.dispatch)

    applyDiff(document.body, main, newMain)
  })
}

store.subscribe(render)

render()
```

Using the Redux's store instead of the Event Bus build in the previous section makes almost no difference to the controller. Furthermore, as you can see in the complete application code,[18] the reducer has exactly the same code as the model from the frameworkless event bus.

One of the main advantages of using Redux instead of a frameworkless event bus is the large number of tools and plugins available. One of the most famous tools for Redux developers is Redux DevTools. Using it, developers can easily log all the actions dispatched in the system and see how they affected the state. Moreover, it is possible to import or export the state in JSON format. Figure 8-8 shows the Redux DevTools in action.

---

[18] https://github.com/Apress/frameworkless-front-end-development/tree/master/Chapter08/04

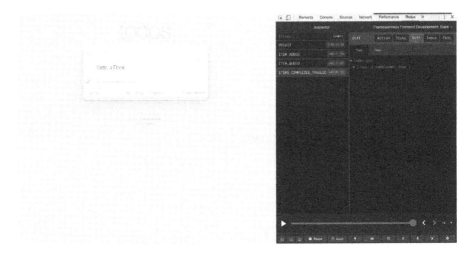

Figure 8-8. *Redux DevTools*

Comparing State Management Strategies

This last section points out the characteristics of the three kinds of state management strategies analyzed in this chapter from three different points of view: *simplicity, consistency,* and *scalability.*

Model View Controller

Model view controller is fairly simple to implement and gives developers a lot of advantages. For example, a good grade of separation of concerns and testability of your domain's business logic.

The real problem of MVC is that it is not a strict pattern. The definition of the elements and the relations between them can be *unclear.* If you ask the question, "What exactly is the difference between the view and the controller?" you can get a lot of different answers. This happens because every MVC framework filled in the "gray areas" of the MVC pattern with their own ideas, so every framework implemented a slightly different version of the MVC. To effectively work with a frameworkless MVC, the first task to is to define your team's MVC rules.

This is also a problem for scalability. When your application grows bigger, the number of "gray areas" grow too, and if the consistency problem is not addressed, your code may become unreadable.

Reactive Programming

The main idea behind *Reactive programming* is that everything in your application is an observable. You saw how easy it is to build observable models, but there are libraries (like RxJS) that transform every aspect of a front-end application to an observable, from user inputs to timers to HTTP requests. This approach guarantees good consistency because you work with objects of the "same type."

Nevertheless, wrapping everything in an observable is not simple. It may become easy if you use a third-party library like RxJS, but that does not mean it would be *simple*.

Caution   Implementing an easy architecture is not the same thing as building a *simple* one. Your goal should be to create the simplest architecture that matches your requirements, not the easiest one to build.

It may not be that simple because you're working with a massive *abstraction*: everything is an observable. Working with abstractions can become a problem when your application becomes bigger, because they start to "leak".[19] *Leakiness* is not a specific problem of Reactive programming; it's related to any pattern (or framework) based on a central abstraction. This is extensively explained by the "Law of Leaky Abstractions," coined by Joel Spolsky, which states:

"All non-trivial abstractions, to some degree, are leaky."

When your application grows, there will be some parts that are not suited for that abstraction and this fact can become a big problem for scalability.

Event Bus

The Event Bus architecture (and in general event-driven architectures) is based on a single, strict rule: "Every state change is generated by an event." This rule helps to keep the complexity of your application proportional to its size, while in other architectures, the complexity is *exponential* to the size of the application. That is one of the reasons that the code of an extensive application is usually less readable than the code of a small one.

This happens because, with the increase in the number of elements that compose your application, there are a lot of possibilities related to how to let them communicate, as shown in Figure 8-9.

---

[19] https://en.wikipedia.org/wiki/Leaky_abstraction

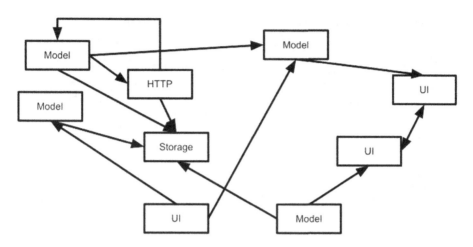

Figure 8-9. *Complexity in a big application*

Strictly following the Event Bus pattern will remove this complexity because the only way to communicate is through the bus itself (compare Figure 8-9 with Figure 8-7). This feature makes Event Bus a very good approach if your first concern is the scalability.

As you saw in the section about the frameworkless implementation of the Event Bus, it's relatively easy to use and build. It's also relatively simple because the abstraction behind the pattern is not as strong as in Reactive programming. The main problem with Event Bus is its verbosity.[20] For every state update, the team needs to create the event, dispatch it through the bus, write the model that updated the state, and finally send the new state to the listeners. Because of the verbosity of this pattern, not all of the application's state is managed with it. In the long run, developers tend to pair it with another state management strategy (such as MVC or Reactive) to manage smaller or simpler domains, resulting in a loss of consistency.

---

[20] For Redux, some specific libraries like https://redux-toolkit.js.org/ are born to solve the verbosity problem.

Table 8-2 is a summary of the comparison made in this section.

Table 8-2. *State Management Strategies Comparison*

	Simplicity	Consistency	Scalability
MVC	✓	✗	✗
Reactive	✗	✓	-
Event Bus	-	✗	✓

As you might have noticed, none of these characteristics is really measurable. They are just my personal thoughts based on my studies and experiences. Using the different patterns covered in this chapter may lead you to completely different considerations.

Summary

In this chapter, you we learned the meaning of state management and why it is important to create in client applications. You then analyzed and implemented three different state management strategies: model view controller, Reactive programming, and Event Bus.

CHAPTER 9

Frameworkless Refactoring: StranglerFigApplication Pattern

Now that you have learned about the five main "blocks" that frameworks provide to build front-end applications—rendering, events, HTTP requests, routing, and state management—the next objective is to cover how to apply these blocks to the existing codebase to replace an old framework. While there are some outstanding books about refactoring and managing legacy code, most of the material I read in my career is about back-end code. The reason is simple: Looking at the big picture of software development history, front-end development is relatively young. So, by some accounts, it is natural that all the material about this topic covers back-end problems.

This chapter explains how to apply one of the most famous refactoring patterns—the StranglerFigApplication—to a front-end application. More specifically, it's about transforming an AngularJS application to a frameworkless one.

© Francesco Strazzullo 2023
F. Strazzullo, *Frameworkless Front-End Development*,
https://doi.org/10.1007/978-1-4842-9351-5_9

Setting the Stage

The story in this chapter is based on a real-life scenario I tackled with my team some years ago. I need to give you some context about the client and their product to understand why we chose to work the way we did. It was 2013, and we collaborated with a new client, helping them create an SPA for their product. They were working on porting a desktop ERP to a web version of the same software. The development of that software was, for them, a market test: They needed to know if their historical client would be interested in working with a web version or if the web version could attract new clients.

So, to be quick in testing this new market, our team needed to be as fast as possible to release a working version of this software. It was 2013, and we used AngularJS: At the time, it was almost a de facto standard for that application.

Fast forward to five years later, in 2018. The web version of the software is a commercial success, the desktop version is only maintained for long-term support, but no new features are planned. Most of the company's efforts shifted to the web version because it became this client's most important source of revenue. At that time, AngularJS started to become a problem; its EOF was arriving and finding people willing to work with it was harder and harder. We decided to find a solution to remove AngularJS from the application, replacing it with something else, but with which framework? When creating the software, our top priority was the time-to-market, but now it was durability. The company was making the bulk of its money with this software, so it should (virtually) last as long as the company itself. The only real durable solution in the 2018 JavaScript ecosystem was a frameworkless approach.

The Solution

We needed to understand how to solve the AngularJS problem and include a frameworkless codebase. A significant rewrite was not an option; the software was too big and the team too small, even if only considering that option. We needed to refactor our codebase one piece at a time, and after some analyses and POCs, we came up with the `StranglerFigApplication`[1] pattern. The main idea is to create a new version of a codebase that, over time, will "strangle" the original application completely. (The name of the pattern came from the Strangler figs plants that operate in a similar way to trees, the figs suck up the nutrients from its victims, causing them to die eventually.)

In the same way, this frameworkless application would strangle the AngularJS one, letting it "die" when all the code was ported from one application to the other. As shown in Figure 9-1, the original application was bundled with Grunt, while the new one was created using Webpack.

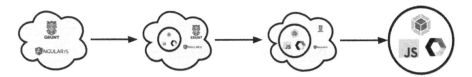

Figure 9-1. *From AngularJS to frameworkless with StranglerApplication*

The Example

Now you will see a near real-world example. This chapter is divided into steps that mimic the refactoring of an actual application. It starts with an AngularJS application, and step by step, you will remove more and more pieces of the original application, substituting them with the frameworkless code.

---

[1] `https://martinfowler.com/bliki/StranglerFigApplication.html`

The Original Application

This application refactors a Twitter clone; the user can read a list of tweets and post a new one. The data that the front-end application consumes is generated by a simple web server[2] based on faker.js.[3] You can see the main page of the app in Figure 9-2.

Figure 9-2. AngularJS application to refactor

The application is relatively straightforward, with two routes formed by a template and a controller. Both controllers use a tweets service to interact with the REST APIs. Listings 9-1 to 9-6 show the whole application codebase.

Listing 9-1. Application Routes Definition

```
angular
  .module('myApp', ['ngRoute'])
```

---

[2]You can see the code on GitHub at https://github.com/Apress/
Frameworkless-Front-End-Development-2nd-ed./blob/main/Chapter09/00/
server/tweets.js)

[3]https://fakerjs.dev/.

```
  .config(['$routeProvider', ($routeProvider) => {
    $routeProvider
      .when('/', {
        templateUrl: 'app/templates/list.tpl.html',
        controller: 'ListController'
      })
      .when('/tweet', {
        templateUrl: 'app/templates/tweet.tpl.html',
        controller: 'TweetController'
      })
      .otherwise({redirectTo: '/'})
  }])
```

Listing 9-2. Tweet List Page Template

```
<div class="container">
    <button class="confirm" data-ng-click="goToNewTweet()">
        New Tweet
    </button>
    <div class="item hoverable" data-ng-repeat="item in list">
        <img class="avatar" ng-src="{{item.avatar}}" />
        <div class="item-content">
            <div>
                <span class="name">{{item.name}}</span>
                <small class="username">{{item.userName}}
                </small>
            </div>
            <div class="tweet">
                {{item.tweet}}
            </div>
        </div>
    </div>
</div>
```

Listing 9-3. Tweet List Page Controller

```
angular
  .module('myApp')
  .controller('ListController', [
    '$scope',
    'tweets',
    '$location', function ($scope, tweets, $location) {
      $scope.list = []
      tweets.list().then((list) => {
        $scope.list = list
      })

      $scope.goToNewTweet = () => {
        $location.path('/tweet')
      }
    }])
```

Listing 9-4. Tweet Detail Page Template

```
<div class="container">
    <div class="item">
        <div class="tweet-form">
            <textarea data-ng-model="tweet" placeholder="write
            your tweet here..." maxlength="140"></textarea>
            <progress value="{{tweet.length}}" max="140">
            </progress>
            <span class="char-count">Characters left:
            {{140 - tweet.length}}</span>
        </div>
    </div>
    <button class="confirm" data-ng-disabled="!tweet"
    data-ng-click="sendTweet()">
```

```
        Send
     </button>
</div>
```

Listing 9-5. Tweet Detail Page Controller

```
angular
  .module('myApp')
  .controller('TweetController', [
    '$scope',
    'tweets',
    '$location',
    function (
      $scope,
      tweets,
      $location
    ) {
      $scope.loading = false
      $scope.tweet = ''

      $scope.sendTweet = () => {
        $scope.loading = true
        tweets.send({
          tweet: $scope.tweet
        }).then(() => {
          $scope.tweet = ''
          $scope.loading = false
          $location.path('/')
        })
      }
    }])
```

Listing 9-6. Tweet API Service

```
angular
  .module('myApp')
  .service('tweets', ['$http', function ($http) {
    const URL = 'http://localhost:3000/api/tweet'
    const list = () => {
      return $http
        .get(URL)
        .then((response) => response.data)
    }
    const send = (data) => {
      return $http
        .post(URL, data)
        .then((response) => response.data)
    }
    return {
      list,
      send
    }
  }])
```

The code shown in the previous listings is quite simple—almost trivial—but I think it is an excellent example of a standard AngularJS application that you can use as a model for a refactoring process.

Moving Services

The first and most important thing to do when modernizing a legacy front-end application is to let new "business logic" be used by the old application. In this example, the only real piece of business logic is the tweets service in Listing 9-6. In Listing 9-7, the same service has been "translated" to a frameworkless approach using fetch.

Listing 9-7. Tweet API Service (Frameworkless Version)

```
const URL = 'http://localhost:3000/api/tweet'

const list = async () => {
  const response = await window.fetch(URL, {
    method: 'GET',
    headers: {
      'Content-Type': 'application/json'
    }
  })
  return response.json()
}

const send = async (data) => {
  const response = await fetch(URL, {
    method: 'POST',
    headers: {
      'Content-Type': 'application/json'
    },
    body: JSON.stringify(data)
  })
  return response.json()
}

const tweets = {
  list,
  send
}

export const angularElement = [() => tweets]

export default tweets
```

The code is relatively straightforward;. Here is only one feature that may seem odd at first glance: The double export at the end of the listing, the default and the named one. The default export is used by all the "new code" based on ES modules, while the angularElement export is used by the "old" AngularJS application (notice the array form typical of AngularJS). But how do you make this service available to AngularJS? The solution is relatively easy, as shown in Listing 9-8.

Listing 9-8. Booting the StranglerFigApplication

```
import {angularElement as tweets} from './services/tweets.mjs'

angular
  .module('myApp')
  .service('tweets', tweets)

const boot = () => {
  angular
    .element(document)
    .ready(() => {
      angular.bootstrap(document, ['myApp'])
    })
}

boot()
```

While the snippet in Listing 9-8 is small, it is essential to understand how this process works. You import the service via the named import and inject it into the AngularJS application. After you import all services, you boot the application. Every service created in the new application is available to both the old application via the named import/inject trick and the new application via standard default export.

> **Note** It is not mandatory to use the default export for the new application; you can use a named export also for the new application. I suggest using the same named export for every module that needs to be ported to the old application in the same way, like the angularElement name used in the previous listings.

Moving Components

The strategy to move UI elements that I prefer when using the StranglerFigApplication pattern is to convert one route (or page) at a time using Web Components, porting all the smaller components that compose the pattern library along the way. Listings 9-9 and 9-10 show the Web Component version of the new tweet page.

Listing 9-9. Tweet Page as a Web Component (JavaScript)

```
import { loadDomElement } from '../utils/rendering.mjs'
import tweets from '../services/tweets.mjs'

class TweetPage extends HTMLElement {
  constructor () {
    super()
    this.tweet = ''
  }

  connectedCallback () {
    window.requestAnimationFrame(() => this.render())
  }

  onChange (value) {
    this.tweet = value
    const {length} = value
```

```
    this.querySelector('my-app-character-counter').
    value = length
    this.querySelector('my-app-progress-bar').value = length
  }

  async send () {
    await tweets.send({
      tweet: this.tweet
    })

    window.location.hash = '/'
  }

  async render () {
    this.innerHTML = ''
    const child = await loadDomElement('./app/es6/components/
    TweetPage.tpl.html')
    this.appendChild(child)

    const textarea = this.querySelector('textarea')

    textarea.value = this.tweet
    textarea.addEventListener('input', e => this.onChange
    (e.target.value))

    this
      .querySelector('button')
      .addEventListener('click', () => this.send())
  }
}

export default TweetPage
```

Listing 9-10. Tweet Page as a Web Component (Template)

```
<div class="container">
    <div class="item">
        <div class="tweet-form">
            <textarea placeholder="write your tweet here..."
            maxlength="140"></textarea>
            <my-app-progress-bar></my-app-progress-bar>
            <my-app-character-counter></my-app-character-
            counter>
        </div>
    </div>
    <button class="confirm" data-ng-disabled="!tweet"
    data-ng-click="sendTweet()">
        Send
    </button>
</div>
```

The code in the previous listing is very similar to the code you analyzed in earlier chapters, so there is no deep analysis of it. The only important thing is that two other components were created while creating my-app-character-counter and my-app-progress-bar. To connect this page to AngularJS, you need two steps—first, register the TweetPage as a Web Component via the custom elements registry with this instruction:

```
window.customElements.define('my-app-tweet-page', TweetPage
```

Then change the AngularJS's route definition to render the newly created page:

```
[...]
.when('/tweet', {
        template: '<my-app-tweet-page></my-app-tweet-page>'
    })
```

This way, one page at a time, you can convert all the applications. This scenario is similar to applying the `StranglerFigApplication` pattern in a back-end application, using a proxy, and then converting one route at a time. In this case, the proxy is the routing system of AngularJS, and the REST API converts the pages of the application.

Other Conversion Strategies

Let's recap how the process explained in this chapter works: You create a second build system, based on ES modules, you connect the new system to the old system, and then you convert one piece of the old application at a time to the new one. You do this until the old application is completely removed or is small enough not to be a problem anymore. Then you can explore some other conversion strategies that can be used to achieve the objective.

iframes

Instead of using modules and pages, your team can create a completely separate application and inject that into the old application via iframes. The two applications can communicate and exchange events or data in different ways, such as by using post messaging.[4]

Proxy

Another option is to keep the two applications completely separated, hosted on two different servers, and put a proxy in front of them. While your team converts the old application, they tell the proxy to switch from

---

[4]https://developer.mozilla.org/en-US/docs/Web/API/Window/postMessage

some routes from the old application to the new one. This approach is particularly beneficial if your team does not need to modify the behavior of the existing application but instead needs to create a new part of the application that could be isolated very quickly.

Summary

This chapter covered how to refactor an application based on an obsolete framework to a frameworkless application using the `StranglerFigApplication` pattern. While the examples shown in this chapter focus on frameworkless code, the same technique could be used to move from one framework to another.

CHAPTER 10

Defending from Frameworks

The previous chapter explored the `StranglerFigApplication` pattern, which is a way to rewrite a legacy application from the inside, substituting new pieces along the usual new feature development flow. This chapter covers how to build an application by mixing frameworkless code and code based on frameworks, as well as how to create a stable codebase that does not need considerable refactoring to remove a framework or parts of it that are no longer required.

Before doing that, I need to explain the meaning of the title of this chapter: *defending from frameworks*. To do that, I want to start with a concept I covered in Chapter 1: technical debt. In a nutshell, technical debt is the difference between the perfect application (from a technical point of view) and your actual codebase. Every shortcut or decision that can give a team a speed boost but sacrifices quality adds something to the heap of technical debt, especially when the code is out of your control. For this reason—not being in control—frameworks can also become a part of technical debt. But, as I briefly explained in Chapter 1, sometimes shortcuts (and frameworks are, in fact, "shortcuts") are necessary to bring a solution to the market in time. In this case, it becomes what I call a "technical investment."

© Francesco Strazzullo 2023
F. Strazzullo, *Frameworkless Front-End Development*,
https://doi.org/10.1007/978-1-4842-9351-5_10

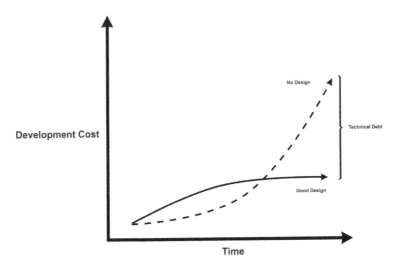

Figure 10-1. *Technical debt*

Now let's try to analyze what "defending from frameworks" means. Defending from what? From over-indebtedness. The phrase "defending from frameworks" suggests that developers should avoid relying too much on frameworks or, to explain my point better, they should avoid relying on all the framework features.

In the next chapter, you learn about a tool that's used to classify frameworks based on whether they are "general purpose" tools. But, as a rule of thumb, frameworks are huge and usually bloated compared to what a development team needs. This chapter and its considerations are critical because going fully frameworkless is—most of the time—not a viable option due to constraints like time, budget, or the need to recruit developers in the market. Working with frameworks should not be considered a black-or-white approach—choosing a framework or going frameworkless—but more as a scale of grays when the team is responsible for defining its strategy, as shown in Figure 10-2.

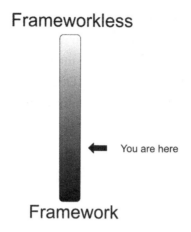

Figure 10-2. *The "defending from framework" strategy*

To conclude, defending from frameworks means carefully choosing which features are useful for your scenario and which just add debt that someone has to pay in the future. I call the "defending from framework" strategy the actual list of features that a team chooses to use and the one they will build from scratch.

Classify Framework Features

Throughout this book, I covered the essential features of front-end frameworks and explained how to implement them with vanilla JavaScript, and this is what I called the "frameworkless toolkit." What I do in this chapter is analyze each of them from two different points of view:

- The amount of debt generated

- The effort required to use a frameworkless solution

This analysis aims to help you define your "strategy" in defending from a framework or, if you prefer, finding your position in Figure 10-2. The analysis of the effort is based on my experiences and the skills of the teams with which I have collaborated over the years. Different teams can incur completely different levels of action. Also, the features I choose to analyze are arbitrary; every team should decide to split up the features based on what they need or want to explore. Some teams may want to question if creating a rendering engine is an option. Other teams that need to rely on some particular protocol for server communication might want to analyze that specific aspect.

Rendering/Event Management

The first analysis covers rendering and event management; while they are two different topics, they need to be considered as one in this scenario. It is challenging—and usually very inefficient—to build a frameworkless event management system on top of an existing rendering framework or vice versa.

Technical Debt: High

Rendering is the core of front-end applications; they live to display data to the user and react to their inputs. This aspect of front-end applications makes the rendering code of a framework the most difficult to "remove," precisely because of the importance of this aspect. Removing the rendering part of a framework means removing the entire framework from the codebase. As explained in Chapter 9, this is no easy task.

Effort: Highest

Rendering is hard. Efficient rendering is even harder. As a rule of thumb, the effort to build a frameworkless rendering engine is high. To evaluate the effort needed to develop your rendering engine, your team should determine the functional requirements of their application. From a rendering point-of-view, building an ERP[1] software with many tables/ detail pages is completely different from creating a real-time chat or a streaming service.

HTTP Request

Technical Debt: Low

As I mentioned in the previous section, front-end applications are all about showing data. Usually, this data comes from a web server via HTTP request, most of the time using the REST architecture with JSON payload. So, receiving and sending asynchronous data is crucial, just like rendering. If the codebase is written using some clean code practice, the HTTP layer should be covered by an anti-corruption layer, hiding the implementation based on frameworks. Just this simple precaution can keep the technical debt under control.

Effort: Lowest

Thanks to the `fetch`[2] API, which is now available on all browsers, creating a frameworkless HTTP requests layer is quite straightforward. Things can become more complicated if you're using GraphQL[3] architecture or your application relies heavily on socket communication.

---

[1] https://en.wikipedia.org/wiki/Enterprise_resource_planning
[2] https://developer.mozilla.org/en-US/docs/Web/API/Fetch_API
[3] https://graphql.org/

Routing

Technical Debt: Medium

Routing is the nervous system of an SPA. When changing the framework in an existing application—or removing it, as in Chapter 9—a team usually works "route by route," changing the application one page at a time. But the piece of a codebase that manages which page is shown at which URL, the routing, is the last piece to be changed. I witnessed some huge refactoring that removed old frameworks almost entirely; the only part left was the routing system. This is usually the case when working on a very large application with hundreds of routes. Changing all of them can become quite challenging. But in any case, the cost of keeping a "zombie" framework just for the routes is manageable.

Effort: Low

The interesting thing about building your routing system is that the complexity of the code is constant; it does not depend on the size of the application. The code shown in Chapter 7 can serve an extensive application without any problem.

State Management

Technical Debt: Highest

State management is where the "magic" happens, where all the code related to a software's specific use cases—generally called the "business logic"—resides. Binding that kind of code to a particular framework skyrockets the technical debt. Suppose the application is big enough and not using techniques like hexagonal architecture.[4] In that case, your business logic will become a mess bundled with framework code, which is incredibly difficult to untangle.

Effort: Low

As demonstrated in Chapter 8, creating a custom state management strategy is quite simple. Actually, it can also be simpler. You can just create simple vanilla JavaScript objects that represent your business logic and link them to the existing framework before building a state management layer for consistency. But a group of POJOs[5] is all a team needs to work with small to medium applications.

Visualizing Your Strategy

As explained, the features analyzed here and the level of effort needed are not written in stone, and they greatly depend on the application to build and on the skill level of the team. But in any case, using the "technical debt" and the "effort" aspects, this section compares every feature and puts them on a map called the *framework strategy map,* as shown in Figure 10-3.

---

[4] https://en.wikipedia.org/wiki/Hexagonal_architecture_(software)
[5] POJO stands for "Plain Old Java Object" but is also used for the JavaScript ecosystem (https://en.wikipedia.org/wiki/Plain_old_Java_object).

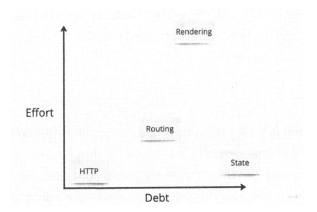

Figure 10-3. *Framework strategy map*

Visualizing framework features on this kind of map makes it easy to compare them and define a strategy at the beginning of developing a new product. A simple—yet very effective—way to create a plan is what I call "cut off and prioritize." The mechanism is straightforward; considering your team skills and constraints like deadline or budget, you draw a horizontal line called the framework cut-off line. The framework will provide everything that is over the line. All the items under the line will be numbered from right to left—from the most high level of debt to the lowest—thus creating a priority. When the team starts working on the product, they will begin working on specific features using those priorities. An example based on the data from Figure 10-3 is shown in Figure 10-4.

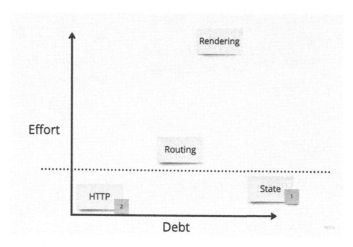

Figure 10-4. *Framework strategy map (2)*

Looking at Figure 10-4, it's quite easy to explain the team's strategy derived from the map:

> "The framework will provide routing and rendering. During development, we will use a state management architecture that we will build. If we have enough time, we will also build the HTTP Request layer, or we will use a dedicated library separated from the original framework."

The real power of these kinds of visual tools is that they can sum up hours of conversation in a couple of seconds. They work much better than pages of documentation when talking about architectural decisions.

Summary

This chapter explored the meaning of "defending from frameworks" and used a simple exercise based on a visual map to define a framework strategy shared by team members.

CHAPTER 11

The Right Tool for the Right Job

Programming is a social activity.

—Robert C. Martin

In the previous chapters, you learned about the frameworkless toolkit pieces. You know how to render DOM elements, manage user input, make HTTP requests, implement a client-side routing system, and manage the state of your application. You're now ready to create a complete frameworkless front-end application from scratch.

This final chapter helps you answer the question, "Now that I can work effectively without frameworks, *when* should I do that?" Or, more generally, "Which framework, if any, should I use for this product?"

In a nutshell, this chapter discusses choosing the right tool for the right job. It will do that by defining a list of principles that you should consider when making a technical decision and a collection of practical tools based on these principles.

© Francesco Strazzullo 2023
F. Strazzullo, *Frameworkless Front-End Development*,
https://doi.org/10.1007/978-1-4842-9351-5_11

JavaScript Fatigue

If you are a front-end developer, you probably heard the expression "JavaScript fatigue". JavaScript fatigue was coined around 2016 to express the frustration generated by the inability to keep up with the latest JavaScript libraries or frameworks. For newcomers, JavaScript fatigue can be very hard to manage; they may feel overwhelmed by all the possibilities.

There are several reasons behind the constant change in the JavaScript ecosystem. The most important is that JavaScript now runs almost everywhere. Besides the browser and its natural environment, JavaScript runs on servers, thanks to Node, and in many other environments like mobile applications, blockchain, IoT, and so on. Jeff Atwood stated in the so-called Atwood's law that:

> *Any application that can be written in JavaScript will eventually be written in JavaScript.*

For now, the rule is still valid. Table 11-1 is a non-comprehensive list of areas (excluded the front-end) where JavaScript could be used; for every area, I also include an example tool with a link to the project's home page.

Table 11-1. *JavaScript Ecosystem Cheat Sheet*

	Tool	Link
Back-end	Node.JS	https://nodejs.org/
Ethereum blockchain	Truffle Suite	https://truffleframework.com/
Mobile applications	React Native	https://facebook.github.io/react-native/
IoT	Johnny-Five	http://johnny-five.io/
NES programming	Nesly	https://github.com/emkay/nesly
Machine learning	TensorFlow	www.tensorflow.org/
Alexa Skill	ASK (Alexa Skill Kit)	https://github.com/alexa/alexa-skills-kit-sdk-for-nodejs

Limiting the reasoning about the "fatigue" only to the front-end, there are a lot of options out there. In addition to the three mainstream frameworks—Angular, React, and Vue—many small libraries solve specific problems. In previous chapters, you learned about some of them, like Redux for state management and Navigo for routing, but they are just the tip of the iceberg.

I don't like the expression "JavaScript fatigue." I am delighted to have a lot of choices in my ecosystem. This book would never have been published if I hadn't had the opportunity to study the code of React, Angular, and so on. Frameworks and libraries are great for learning. So, the more frameworks you have, the faster you can learn new paradigms, and the competition between libraries raises the bar, feature by feature. I love to call this period the "JavaScript Renaissance," a great moment to be a JavaScript developer.

The "Right" Framework

Why did I start this chapter with a section about the JavaScript Renaissance? Because with the fantastic opportunities this ecosystem gives developers also comes a challenge: Choosing the suitable framework. I hope that this chapter can help you and your team with this task. Remember that whenever I discuss choosing a framework, I always put a frameworkless option on the table.

Tip   When choosing a framework, always consider a frameworkless option. You may notice that frameworks are not giving you any advantage in that particular scenario.

With "choose," I don't mean just to select a framework from a list but to analyze and apply some decision-making techniques in a structured way. Because of the magnitude of the decision-making topic, this chapter introduces some basic principles that should drive you to choose a framework. If you want to study decision-making in depth, here are some books that I suggest you read:

- *Decision Making For Dummies* by Dawna Jones (`www.amazon.com/Decision-Making-Dummies-Dawna-Jones/dp/111883366X`)

- *The Thinker's Toolkit: 14 Powerful Techniques for Problem-Solving* by Morgan D. Jones (`www.amazon.com/Thinkers-Toolkit-Powerful-Techniques-Problem/dp/0812928083`)

- *Thinking, Fast and Slow* by Daniel Kahneman (`www.amazon.com/Thinking-Fast-Slow-Daniel-Kahneman/dp/0374533555`)

What does the "right" framework mean? One of the definitions that you may find in the dictionary states:

True or correct as a fact.

But can a framework be correct as a "fact"? I don't think so. There is probably more than one "right" framework for your project. So I will change the challenge from "choosing the right framework" to "choosing a good enough framework." By good enough, I mean one that helps your team achieve its goals.

Tip   If a framework seems good enough, you should stop searching. Trying to find the perfect match may cost you a lot of time.

So, throughout the rest of this chapter, I talk about "how to choose a good enough framework" instead of the differences between React, Angular, and so on. I do that because I firmly agree with one of the main points of the Agile Manifesto:[1]

> *Individuals and interactions over processes and tools.*
>
> —Agile Manifesto

In other words, I want to focus on the team making that decision and how they interact. Therefore, the challenge becomes "choosing a good enough framework in the right way."

The Frameworkless Manifesto

As explained in the front matter, this book is related to the frameworkless movement: A group of developers interested in developing without frameworks and in making mindful technical decisions. In the Manifesto[2] of the Movement, you can find the principles that drive the people who believe in the frameworkless movement when making technical decisions.

This section analyzes these principles, explaining how they can be useful in your day-by-day job.

The First Principle

The first principle states that:

> *The value of software is not the code itself but in the reasons behind the existence of that code.*

---

[1] https://agilemanifesto.org/
[2] https://github.com/frameworkless-movement/manifesto

In other words, to make mindful decisions about software (like choosing a framework), you should clarify the reasons that a team is building software in the first place. A way to know these reasons is to consult the Business Model Canvas (BMC) of your project. A BMC is a way to visually represent how the company wants to make money from your software. You can download an empty Canvas at this website,[3] and if you want more information, you can read the book, *Business Model Generation,* by Alexander Osterwalder and Yves Pigneur.[4]

This canvas is composed of nine "blocks" that, when filled, give a lot of information at a glance. For example:

- **Customer segments**: Which customers your company is trying to serve

- **Value proposition**: The products (or services) that your company offers to meet the needs of the customers

- **Key activities**: The essential activities needed to develop the value proposition

- **Key resources**: The necessary resources to develop the value proposition

As you may imagine, your technical decisions should be influenced by the information that you get from the BMC.

Tip   If your company does not have a BMC for your project, try to create one. It contains a lot of helpful information.

---

[3] www.strategyzer.com/canvas/business-model-canvas

[4] www.amazon.com/Business-Model-Generation-Visionaries-Challengers/dp/0470876417

The Second Principle

The second principle states that:

> *Every decision should be made considering the context. A good choice in a given context could be a bad choice in another one.*

This principle may seem quite apparent at first, but the main problem is to define the "context" of a software. A method that I find really compelling is to use a list of non-functional requirements (NFR). We all know what a functional requirement is: A way to define what the software should do. Usually, they come in the form of user stories; for example:

> *As an **anonymous user**, I want to **log in**, so that **I can access the premium area**.*

NFRs are a way to define how a software should be instead of what it should do. Take a look at this second version of the user story:

> *As an anonymous user, I want to log in, so that I can access the premium area **in less than one second.***

As you can see, in this new version of the user story, it's beneficial to understand if you are doing a good job developing the Login feature of the software. In this case, the software should be performant enough to let the users log in in less than one second. Table 11-2 shows a non-comprehensive list of NFRs; for a complete list, you can consult Wikipedia's entry about non-functional requirements.[5]

---

[5] https://en.wikipedia.org/wiki/Non-functional_requirement

Table 11-2. *Partial List of NFRs*

Accessibility	Maintainability	Extensibility
Performances	Wow-Effect	Portability
Evolvability	Customizability	Testability
Deployability	Credibility	Reusability

The NFRs are a crucial aspect to keep in mind when making any kind of technical decision. Two software programs with the exact functional requirements but different NFRs need different technologies. Alas, NFRs are usually entirely ignored when describing software.

Caution   You can't rely only on functional requirements to make mindful technical decisions. Keep NFRs in mind as well.

The Third Principle

The third principle states:

The mindful choice of a framework is a technical one and should be made by technical people, taking business needs into account.

This is a critical point. Choosing a framework is a technical decision, and so is a responsibility of a technical team. But to make a mindful decision, you must consider business needs. For example, if you work for a startup, shortening the time to market (TTM) is crucial to get customer feedback. You need to reach a compromise between quality and the velocity required for a short TTM.

The Fourth Principle

The fourth principle states:

> *The decision-making criteria that led to the choice of a framework should be known to all the members of the team.*

This last principle is not directly related to "how" to make technical decisions. Nevertheless, it's a very important one. All the members (not just developers) of your team should know the criteria that led to a particular decision. This is very important because, after some time, it's hard to judge the result of a decision without knowing the original context. When somebody enters a brownfield project, they usually have a lot of questions about the architecture and tools chosen to work. Without knowing the criteria that brought the team to that decision, they are blind. They can mindlessly accept the decisions without questioning them, or they can mindlessly change them. Both of these scenarios are far from ideal; developers should not make any kind of decisions blindly.

A beneficial tool that tries to address these problems is the Lightweight Architecture Decision Records (LADR). LADR is a way, developed by Michael Nygard,[6] to keep track of all the meaningful decisions that are made during the lifespan of a project. For every architectural decision that the team make, an Architectural Decision Record (ADR) is created.

---

[6] http://thinkrelevance.com/blog/2011/11/15/documenting-architecture-decisions

This ADR is a numbered markdown file that should be kept in the project repository. You can see an example of ADR on GitHub.[7] Every ADR should contain the following:

- Title

- Context (discussing, accepted, deprecated, superseded)

- Decision

- Status

- Consequences

None of these ADRs should be deleted, even if the decision that they talk about is not valid anymore. In that case, a new ADR is created to state the new decision and the status of the old one is changed to superseded. When a new member of the team enters the project, they should read all the ADRs present in the repository.

Tools

This section covers a very small collection of technical decision-making tools that you can start using every time you need to choose whether to work with a framework.

---

[7]https://github.com/Apress/Frameworkless-Front-End-Development-2nd-ed./blob/main/Chapter11/ADR-001.MD

Matteo Vaccari's Tool

This tool,[8] created by my friend Matteo Vaccari, is handy for classifying a list of libraries/frameworks that you're evaluating for your project. Place every library on a two-axis graph, like the one shown in Figure 11-1.

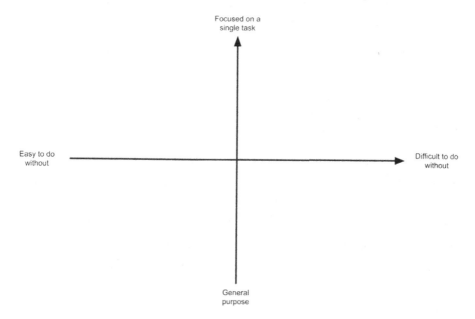

Figure 11-1. *Matteo Vaccari's tool*

After you place all the elements on the graph, you can use the tool to develop a strategy:

- **Upper-left quadrant**: These elements are good candidates for a frameworkless approach if you have the time to build the same features from scratch.

- **Upper-right quadrant**: These elements should be included in your codebase. Nevertheless, remember to write an interface around them.

---

[8]http://matteo.vaccari.name/blog/archives/1022

- **Lower-right quadrant**: You may decide to add them to the codebase or to study them in order to move them to the lower-left quadrant.

- **Lower-left quadrant**: You should avoid putting them in the codebase. If something is general purpose, it's usually hard to remove later.

Of course, what you just read is not a strict rule. There might be exceptions that you need to discuss with your team.

Trade-off Sliders

This tool helps your team visualize the context of your software which, as covered in the previous section, is an essential element to making mindful decisions. When working with this tool, the first task is to choose four or five metrics that you want to compare. Most of the time, I use Quality, Scope, Budget, and Deadline, but you can select other metrics if you think that they can be helpful for your project. After that, order these metrics by decreasing "negotiability." You may need to sacrifice the other ones to protect the metrics you put on the top of the list.

Start with a silent voting phase, where each person writes their list and then starts a discussion to reach a consensus on the final list. You should obtain something similar to Figure 11-2.

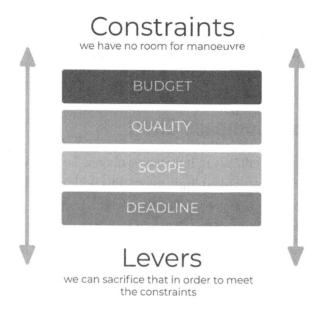

Figure 11-2. *Trade-off slider*

When using this tool, you should also involve your managers. You need their point of view on these metrics, and they need to *understand* that in order to achieve something, you need to sacrifice something else. The name "trade-off sliders" is not accidental; every decision is usually the result of a trade-off of different aspects.

This simple "game" gives the team a lot of helpful information about frameworks. If your first concern is the deadline, you probably have to choose the framework your team knows better. This version of the trade-off sliders differs slightly from the standard one; you can read about the original one on Atlassian's website.[9]

---

[9]`www.atlassian.com/team-playbook/plays/trade-off-sliders`

Tip   Every project has its trade-offs. Use this tool to visualize them and help all the members of the team act accordingly.

Architecture Compass Chart

I created this tool specifically to help teams choose frameworks. It helps to visualize your project's most important NFRs and their relationship. This tool is meant to put together developers and managers in the same meeting, just like trade-off slides. The first step is to choose the five most important NFRs and place them on a radar chart, as shown in Figure 11-3.

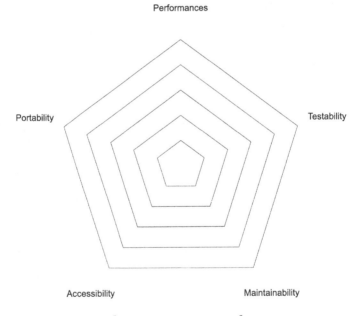

Figure 11-3. *Empty architecture compass chart*

There are different ways to choose the NFRs to put on the chart. Table 11-3 shows some of the tools that I use with links to instructions.

Table 11-3. *Tools to Choose NFRs*

Tool	Link
Agile retrospective	`www.atlassian.com/team-playbook/plays/retrospective`
SWOT analysis	`www.mindtools.com/pages/article/newTMC_05.htm`
Impact mapping	`www.impactmapping.org/`
Lego serious play	`www.lego.com/en-us/seriousplay`

Now you have to vote the importance of each NFRs on the chart (voting from 1 to 5), reaching consensus among the team. You may use a technique similar to the planning poker.[10] Each person calls their vote simultaneously, and then people with high and low votes talk to justify their vote. Then repeat this procedure until you reach a consensus. The result of these votes should be placed on the chart, as in Figure 11-4.

---

[10] `https://en.wikipedia.org/wiki/Planning_poker`

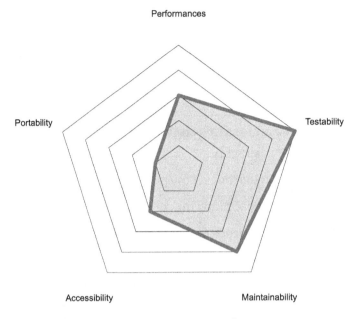

Figure 11-4. *Filled architecture compass chart*

The technical team can now use this chart as a "compass" to choose a framework. For each framework that they want to evaluate, they can create a new chart and see how it fits on the compass, as shown in Figure 11-5.

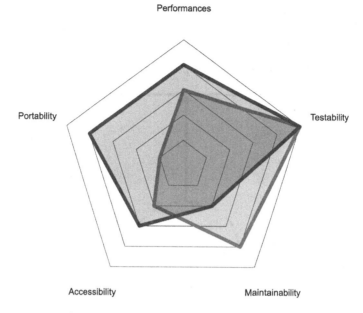

Figure 11-5. *Architecture compass chart with a fitness check*

The most crucial advantage of this tool is to drive the discussion of the tech team toward topics that are useful for the project. In a lot of teams that I helped, everyone was talking about performance. When I talked with the managers, they said that performance was unimportant for their customer segments. This tool helps to avoid these anti-patterns.

Other Tools

There are many other tools you can use when choosing a framework or making any other technical decision. These tools should gather information from these four areas:

- Identity ("who are we?")

- Market ("who are our users?")

- Value ("what should the software do?")

- Context ("How should the software be?")

Figure 11-6 shows the relationship between these areas and decisions.

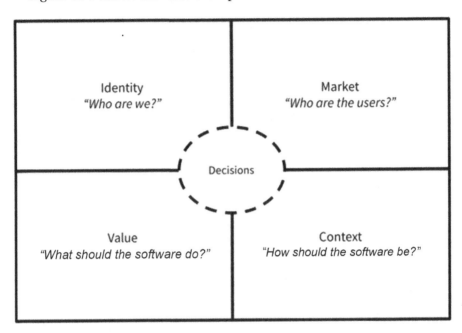

Figure 11-6. *Technical decision-making landscape*

Table 11-4 shows a list of tools. Some of them were covered in the previous sections of this chapter.

Table 11-4. *Decision-Making Tools*

Area	Tool	Link
Identity	Elevator Pitch	www.atlassian.com/team-playbook/plays/elevator-pitch
	Five Whys Analysis	www.atlassian.com/team-playbook/plays/5-whys
	Delegation Board	https://management30.com/practice/delegation-poker/
	Stakeholder Map	www.lucidchart.com/blog/how-to-do-a-stakeholder-analysis
Market	Business Model Canvas	www.strategyzer.com/canvas/business-model-canvas
	Customer Interview	www.atlassian.com/team-playbook/plays/customer-interview
	Customer Journey Mapping	www.atlassian.com/team-playbook/plays/customer-journey-mapping
	Value Proposition Canvas	www.strategyzer.com/canvas/value-proposition-canvas
Value	Event Storming	www.eventstorming.com/
	Impact Mapping	www.impactmapping.org/
	Lean Value Tree	https://blog.avanscoperta.it/it/2018/08/17/product-discovery-orchestrating-experiments-at-scale/
	User Story Mapping	www.jpattonassociates.com/user-story-mapping/

(*continued*)

Table 11-4. (*continued*)

Area	Tool	Link
Context	Trade-off Sliders	`www.atlassian.com/team-playbook/plays/trade-off-sliders`
	Architecture Compass Chart	`https://medium.com/flowingis/framework-compass-chart-d3851c25b45d`
	SWOT Analysis	`www.mindtools.com/pages/article/newTMC_05.htm`

Summary

This last chapter talked about the importance of decision-making principles when choosing a framework or making any other technical decision. You explored some technical decision-making anti-patterns and the problems that they can bring to your organization. The chapter analyzed the principle behind the frameworkless movement and talked about some tools that can help you and your team make mindful technical decisions.

Index

Printed in the United States
by Baker & Taylor Publisher Services